# An Insider's Guide to Provence

Keith Van Sickle

*To Mom and Dad*

*who shared their love of travel with me*

# ALSO BY KEITH VAN SICKLE

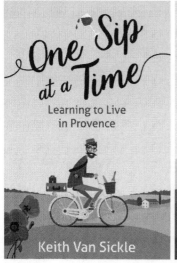
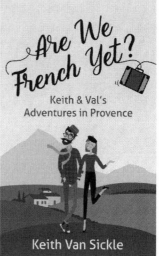

*When the Good Lord begins to doubt the world,*

*he remembers that he created Provence.*

Frédéric Mistral

# Contents

# List of Maps

# A Note from the Author

My wife Val and I live part of the year in Provence. Our first visit was nearly 30 years ago, and it was love at first sight. We started coming every chance we got and finally, about a dozen years ago, we began living here part-time.

We tried living in different parts of Provence—it's a big place, and very diverse—and finally settled on the town of St-Rémy-de-Provence. You might have heard of it, it's where Vincent van Gogh was in a mental asylum and painted masterpieces like *The Starry Night*.

When you live in a place, even part-time like we do, you really get to know it. You discover great local wineries and out-of-the-way restaurants. You find beautiful hiking trails and quiet picnic spots. Your French friends introduce you to their favorite places and they become yours, too.

This book is about the things we love to see and do, our favorite restaurants and wineries, plus some background information on Provence's history and culture. I share both popular places and "insider secrets." The book includes links to lots of articles and websites, in case you'd like to learn more about a particular subject.

Val and I live in the western part of Provence, north of Marseille, so most of this book is about that area. I've written an entire section on St-Rémy, the town where we live, and another on the immediately surrounding area. I highlight our favorites in major regions like the Luberon Valley and cities like Aix-en-Provence, but the coverage is thinner the further east you go. Take a look at the Table of Contents to make sure this book gives you what you are looking for.

Here's something important: *this is not a general guidebook*. For example, it offers no information on lodging. There are many excellent guidebooks out there already, like those I list in the Resources section. Instead, this book is a *supplement* to those general guidebooks, the personal favorites of an American couple living in Provence. I hope it helps make your next trip here a little more special.

Bon voyage!

Keith

p.s. I'd love to hear from you! If you have any comments about this book or suggestions for a future edition, or you'd like to tell me that something in the book is out of date, please contact me at author@keithvansickle.com.

# PROVENCE REGIONS

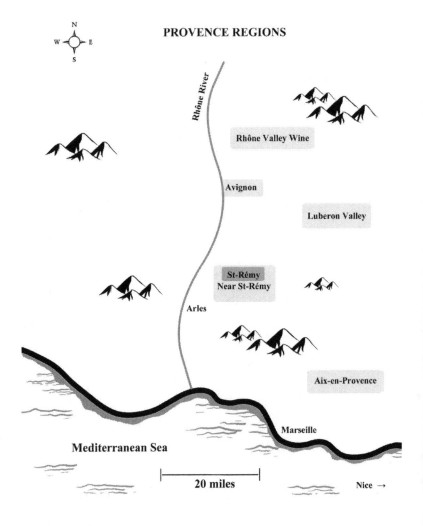

# How to Use This Book

## How the Book is Organized

This guidebook includes both background information—like the section on Provençal culture—and descriptions of things to see and do. These latter are organized by region, with sections on Avignon, the Luberon Valley, the Rhône Valley Wine Country, and more. I've also included sections on two subjects that span regions: Roman Provence and Jewish Provence. Please see the table of contents for more detail.

## What the Book Covers

Provence is big—about the size of Maryland—and this book is weighted towards the areas we know best, in the western part of Provence. There is, for example, an entire section devoted to our adopted hometown of St-Rémy-de-Provence, and another on the immediately surrounding area. As you get further from St-Rémy, especially to the east and places like the Riviera, there is less information.

As this book is a collection of personal favorites, my wife and I have seen and done just about everything in it. I say "just about everything" because there are a few places we haven't yet visited, like the new underwater museum of Marseille, but I've researched them and they sound so cool I've included them anyway.

## Important Items

When there is something I want to draw your attention to, like how to find the entrance to a hidden parking lot, I've highlighted it in **bold**.

## Maps and Links

This book is designed to be used while you are on the go. To take full advantage of its features, you will need the Google Maps app on your phone or tablet. Depending on what kind of device you have, this should be available at Apple's App Store or Google Play.

There are hundreds of links in the book, so if you want to know more about a certain subject, or see it on Google Maps, just follow the appropriate link. The links to maps are identified by this symbol ⊕. You can either type the link into your device (I've made them as short as possible) or you can find the full list of links at keithvansickle.com/Links, where you can just click on them.

I take you to English-language sites wherever possible, but sometimes the only thing available is in French.

## About Us

The book includes a number of favorite hiking and biking routes, so I should tell you that Val and I are in our 60s. We're reasonably active, but not what you would call athletes. There's no danger of us biking to the top of Mont Ventoux! So, when I say that a route is "easy," for example, it means it is easy for us.

## Resources for Planning Your Trip

Be sure to check out the sections Tips on Traveling in Provence and Provençal Culture—they'll help you make the most of your time in Provence. And the Resources section has useful information that can help you plan your trip.

# Tips on Traveling in Provence

## Slow Down

Some vacations are for seeing the sights. Who can visit Paris without gawking at the Eiffel Tower, the Louvre, Versailles, and all the rest? When you go to a place like that, you rush around a lot, and that's ok. But that's not how you should visit Provence.

Sure, there are must-see sights in Provence, but what makes it special is the ambiance, the slow pace, the pleasure of small things. In Provence, start your day with a leisurely coffee and croissant at the local café. Then go to an outdoor market and poke around, tasting here and sampling there. Or perhaps spend the day in a charming little village, lingering over lunch and having that extra glass of wine.

I like to say that Provence moves at the pace of the seasons rather than the speed of the internet. Things often take longer than planned, and a day with several activities rarely happens. So minimize your expectations and be open to the unexpected!

## The Best Time to Visit

For the French, vacations are sacred, right up there with God and motherhood. And summer is vacation season, when many *français* head south in search of sun and sand. They're not alone: people come to the South of France from all over the world.

Provence is glorious in the summer, with the lavender in bloom and the *cigales* chanting. And if you like hot weather, summertime is definitely for you. But my favorite time is during the shoulder seasons—in the spring from early April to mid-June, and in the fall from late August to early October. The weather is cooler then, there are fewer people, and prices are lower.

*Pro tip:* Summer is the busiest time in Provence, and the fall tourist season picks up in September. Most people don't know that the French school year starts at the beginning of September, so the French finish their summer vacations about a week earlier. This creates a secret little quiet period during the last week of August, ideal for a visit.

## The Outdoor Markets

Outdoor markets are one of the glories of France, and Provence has some of the best. Every town has a weekly market, even the smallest village, so you are spoiled for choice. Do you want a big, sprawling market, a cozy little one, or maybe an afternoon market where farmers bring their produce directly from the fields? Do you want food, crafts, clothing, or would you perhaps like to do some antique shopping? You can find everything you want in Provence. There's nothing better than wandering through a Provençal market, taking in the sights and smells…and don't forget to taste!

## Use the Magic Word

When I was a kid, Mom would remind me to "use the magic word!" when I forgot to say please. And while please and thank you are important in France, **the real magic word is** *bonjour* (hello). It is by far the most important word you need to know.

Before you ask the sales clerk for a baguette at the local boulangerie, you say *bonjour*. When you stop a French person on the street to ask for directions, you start with *bonjour* (yes, even before "excuse me.") When you walk into any shop you say *bonjour*, even if you don't see anyone. There's even a complicated protocol around saying *bonjour* at the doctor's office*!

Not saying *bonjour* is considered so rude that some people will ignore you if you don't say it. It's like you don't exist.

## Emergency Numbers

Heaven forbid you should have an emergency while traveling in France, but in case you do, here are important phone numbers to know. These numbers are free of charge and are available 24/7.

---

\*    tinyurl.com/4uhxaks8

## 112 Emergency

Call this if you are the victim of, or the witness to, an accident. This number works in all countries of the European Union.

## 114 Emergency for Deaf and Hard-of-Hearing People

Call this if you are a victim of, or witness to, an emergency situation or accident and require emergency assistance. This number can be accessed by text and fax.

## 15 Medical

This is the emergency medical assistance number. You can use it to call out a medical team to a medical emergency, or to be referred to a round-the-clock medical facility.

## 17 Police

This is to report a crime requiring an immediate police response.

## 18 Fire

To report a dangerous situation or accident concerning people or property and receive a swift response.

# Shopping

## Prepare to Wait

If you go to a shop frequented by the locals, **don't be in a rush**. Everyone gets personal attention and takes as long as they want, which can sometimes be a long time.

In our butcher shop, for example, the butcher takes the time to chat with the local customers. How's the family? How are your bunions? How will you prepare the stew?

Val and I once walked in and found two customers ahead of us. She turned to me and said, "Ok, this will take about 45 minutes." This can sometimes be annoying, but on the other hand we've gotten great recipes and cooking advice, and once in a while some juicy local gossip.

If you don't have time for this, you can usually find faster lines at large stores like *hypermarchés* (supermarkets).

## Paying

Credit cards are accepted almost everywhere, and many vendors now use "touchless" technology for payments up to 50 euro. Beyond that, you'll need to do it the old-fashioned way and sign the receipt. Europeans have credit cards that allow you to enter a code rather than signing the receipt, so sometimes you'll be asked to enter a code because the vendor thinks you have a European card. When this happens to me, I usually pantomime signing a piece of paper and the vendor understands that I have an American credit card and don't have a code, so they print out the receipt.

## French Shopping Carts

If you want to use a shopping cart at a big store like a supermarket, **you'll need a 1-euro coin.** The carts are all locked together and the coin will unlock the one at the end. You put the coin in the slot and it releases a key. The key is attached to a chain, but now that it is disconnected from your cart you are good to go.

When you finish shopping, take the cart back to where you found it. Slide the key into an open slot. Out will pop a 1-euro coin and you are on your way.

If this isn't clear, just watch another shopper. But don't forget that 1-euro coin!

## Bring Your Own Bags

Like many countries, France now encourages shoppers to bring reusable bags to put their purchases in. If you have some, great. If you don't, that's not a problem because the store will have some for you to use (either reusable or temporary), but be aware that you will have to pay for them.

## Learn the Pharmacy Rules

If you need something from a pharmacy, you're in luck because French pharmacies are everywhere, kind of like Starbucks in America. I wouldn't say that French people are hypochondriacs (well, maybe they are) but it's true that they take more prescription drugs than anyone in Europe. The upside of all those pharmacies is that they can be very helpful if you have a medical problem. Seeing a French pharmacist is much easier than getting a doctor's appointment, and can sometimes let you avoid having to see a doctor at all.

Besides prescription drugs, you can find the usual drugstore items at a French pharmacy—shampoo, toothpaste, that sort of thing. You grab them off the shelf and pay, same as at home. But over-the-counter drugs are different. For those, you have to wait in line to see a pharmacist, and then describe your problem so that he or she can dole out the appropriate medication, even if you already know what you need.

This wouldn't be a big deal except that French pharmacies are usually small, which means that everyone in line can hear what you're saying. This can feel embarrassing but don't worry, no one seems to care.

For a very helpful list of common over-the-counter medications and their French equivalents, check out this article[*].

***Pro tip:*** Don't buy Vaseline unless you desperately need it. I bought some once for dry skin on my elbows. Big mistake! I later learned that in France, Vaseline is used for one thing and one thing only: as a sex aid. So, when I said I needed Vaseline, everyone stared at me like I was a sex fiend. Even the pharmacist! Don't let this happen to you.

---

[*]   tinyurl.com/2y9mcj7v

# Dining

## Don't Miss the Specialties

Every region of France has its special foods and Provence is no different. Here are some of my favorites.

### Bouillabaisse

This classic fish stew originated in Marseille and now is famous all over the world. But you have to be careful when you make it, because it can explode[*].

### *Le Grand Aïoli*

Aïoli is a garlicky mayonnaise and *Le Grand Aïoli* is a tempting spread of fish, hard boiled eggs, potatoes, and steamed vegetables, served with a generous dollop of aïoli. For centuries, this was the Friday meal in Catholic Provence, the day when meat was prohibited, and many restaurants still offer *Le Grand Aïoli* as a Friday special.

---

[*]   tinyurl.com/ydeqrh37

## Olives and Olive Oil

Provence is an important center of olive growing and you'll see olive groves everywhere. My favorite varieties are the picholine and the lucques, but all are good. Local oil does well in world competitions, sometimes bringing home the title of World's Best Olive Oil.

## The Spreads

With so many olives in Provence, every market offers olive-based spreads that are delicious on bread or crackers. Don't miss tapenade (black or green olives with a bit of anchovy) and pistounade (green olives with pesto). You can also try caviar d'aubergine (eggplant spread) and anchoïade (lots of anchovies, so this isn't for everyone.)

## Lamb

The best lamb in France comes from Provence and a favorite preparation is *gigot d'agneau* (leg of lamb), traditionally served at Easter but delicious all year round.

## Socca

Socca is a kind of thin, crispy crêpe made out of chickpeas, sprinkled with salt and drizzled with olive oil. It's the sort of thing you munch on while you are having a glass of wine with friends. There's a short movie about socca online, with a fun trailer[*].

---

[*]    tinyurl.com/5zum2j9z

## Ratatouille

Originally from Nice, ratatouille combines some of the fresh produce that Provence is famous for, like tomato, eggplant, zucchini, garlic, and onion.

## Roast Chicken

You'll often see chickens roasting on a spit at an outdoor market, or spinning away in front of a butcher shop. The smell is divine and there's nothing better than a hot roast chicken for a casual meal.

## *Melon de Cavaillon*

There are lots of melons in France but the best* and most famous come from the town of Cavaillon. Be sure to try one if you see them in the market. The citizens of Cavaillon are so proud of their melons that they've even erected a giant melon statue at the entrance to town!

---

**Pastis**

Ok, this isn't for everyone, but if you like black licorice, you have to try pastis. It's the ultimate Provençal drink, the one you see the old fellows drinking while they play pétanque. When you order it, you'll get a glass partly filled with pastis, plus a small pitcher of cold water, and you dilute it to taste (a 4:1 ratio of water to pastis is typical.) I also like to add ice. *Santé!*

## Order Coffee the French Way

You might be surprised when you order coffee and the waiter brings you a tiny cup of very strong brew. "Wait," you think, "I didn't order espresso!" But you did, because a standard French *café* is what other people call espresso. If what you really want is a larger, less intense cup of coffee, you should order a *café américain* (sometimes called a *café filtré* or *café longue*.) Or if you want a cup even stronger than a regular *café*, ask for a *ristretto* or a *café serré*.

Confused? There's a good article* that will help you understand the different kinds of French coffee drinks and how to order them, from a *café au lait* in the morning to a *noisette* after lunch.

---

\*    tinyurl.com/tfh8mpwe

## Find the Best Bakeries

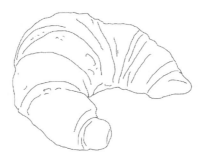

There are thousands of *boulangeries* in France, offering a wide range of breads and pastries. By law, their bread has to be made by hand and on site. But this law doesn't apply to *pâtisseries* and *viennoiseries*—those pastries and quiches and croissants we love so much. As a result, many *boulangeries* buy these items frozen, from big industrial suppliers, and bake them on site. *Quelle horreur!*

Luckily, the French national baker's association has created a new certification process for the boulangeries that produce their goodies the right way. To find one, **look for the *Boulanger de France* logo**, which will be prominently displayed. Here's an article* where you can see the logo and learn what it takes to become a *Boulanger de France.*

---

* tinyurl.com/2fj7h3rb

## Picnic French-Style

Provence is so beautiful that it practically begs you to go on a picnic (or as the French say, *un pique-nique.*) And with all the outdoor markets full of good things to eat, it's easy to put together a memorable meal.

How do the French like to picnic?[*] They keep things simple, typically with just an aperitif (*apéro*), a main course, and dessert. And they never forget the holy trinity of French food: bread, cheese, and wine. Sometimes that's enough!

## Let a Master Chef Cook for You

In 2007, the French government created the title *Maître Restauranteur* (Master Restauranter) to recognize top chefs. Ok, not the super top chefs, the ones with the Michelin stars, but Michelin-starred restaurants are for special occasions. Restaurants with a *Maître Restauranteur* serve excellent food at a reasonable price.

---

[*]  tinyurl.com/ycb2rnsp

To earn the title you must not only be highly skilled, but everything must be homemade, not purchased and reheated.

You can find a *Maître Restauranteur* near you by using the interactive map on their association's website.[*]

## Avoid Allergens

All **restaurants in Europe are required to list the allergens** contained in their dishes, a total of 14 in all. You can refer to this list as you decide what dishes are safe for you to eat. It's usually at the back of the menu, but if you don't see it, ask your server for a copy.

Here are the 14 allergens, and there is a website[†] with a complete description of each one.

1. Gluten
2. Crustaceans
3. Eggs
4. Fish
5. Peanuts
6. Soybeans
7. Milk
8. Certain nuts
9. Celery

---

[*] tinyurl.com/yetsxs3n
[†] tinyurl.com/46t8nvvf

10. Mustard
11. Sesame seeds
12. Sulphur dioxide and sulphites
13. Lupin
14. Molluscs

Please see the sections below for more specific information about avoiding gluten, and about vegan and vegetarian dining.

## Avoid Gluten (for the gluten-intolerant)

Some people have a problem with gluten. I have celiac disease, which prevents me from eating even tiny amounts of the stuff. So how do the gluten-intolerant eat safely in France? Here are some suggestions[*].

Unless you speak good French, bring a French-language restaurant card[†]. Restaurant servers in France often

---

[*]    tinyurl.com/yckpb24f
[†]    tinyurl.com/7d92byrr

speak some English but it's best to be clear with such an important subject.

All **restaurants in Europe are required to list the allergens** contained in their dishes, a total of 14 in all, so you can refer to this list as you decide what to eat. It's usually at the back of the menu, but if you don't see it, ask your server for a copy. See the section above for the full list of allergens.

Smaller restaurants are a good choice for dining gluten-free. These are often family run, with one spouse running the kitchen and the other the dining room. If you need to ask a specific question about a dish, you have a direct line to the kitchen. This is helpful when dealing with things like cross-contamination.

Tell the restaurant about any food restrictions when making your reservation, because it allows them to prepare. If you have given them a heads-up, they'll sometimes have gluten-free bread for you.

If you are shopping* in a supermarket, look for the section marked *Sans Gluten* (gluten free.) Most big supermarkets have one. You'll usually find a better selection, however, in the *bio* (organic food) stores. These are common in France, with nationwide chains like *Naturalia* and *La Vie Claire.*

Foods that are certified gluten free are marked with a special symbol. And if you are reading labels for

---

\*     tinyurl.com/2p9afnss

ingredients, three key words to know are *blé* (wheat), *orge* (barley) and *seigle* (rye.)

There's a searchable list of 100% gluten-free restaurants worldwide that's very useful when traveling[*].

## Eating Vegan or Vegetarian

Many French don't understand the whole "non-meat" thing. If you say you are vegetarian, you will sometimes get a response like "so you eat fish, right?" But things are getting better. Here are some tips that can help.

Two words you'll need to know are *végétalien* (vegan) and *végétarien* (vegetarian.)

When looking for a restaurant, TripAdvisor can be helpful because it allows you to filter for restaurants that provide vegetarian or vegan options. When you are in the restaurant section of TripAdvisor for a particular town, the filters are on the left side of the screen.

For more specific advice, here are some good articles about vegan dining[†] and vegetarian dining[‡] in France.

---

[*]   tinyurl.com/twdrcb98

[†]   tinyurl.com/979kdt8w

[‡]   tinyurl.com/he6z38c8

# Driving

## A Special Auto Lease Program

If you are staying in France for more than three weeks, there is a program available to non-European visitors that could save you money[*].

It's a special leasing program and there's a lot to like about it. First, you get a brand-new car that you choose ahead of time. Second, insurance is included, with zero deductible. Third, cars with automatic transmissions don't cost a lot more than those with manual transmissions, as is usually the case with rentals. AND the car comes with a cool red license plate!

---

[*]    tinyurl.com/y8kqwb8z

## French Gas Stations

Some French cars use diesel fuel rather than unleaded gas, and it is important to keep them straight. Putting the wrong fuel in a car can ruin its engine, and ruin your vacation.

Diesel fuel is marked *Diesel* or *Gazole* and the pump handles are black. (**note:** not all gas stations carry diesel fuel.) Unleaded fuel is marked *Sans Plomb* and the pump handles are green.

You can usually pay at the pump using your credit card, but if your card doesn't have the right microchip in it, it won't work. If this is the case, you can pay inside the gas station, usually before you pump. But don't worry, today most credit cards have microchips that work in French gas stations.

Some gas stations have little pay booths near the exit, though this is becoming rare. If you are in one of these, pump your gas, remember your pump number, and pay on your way out. However, these pumps are only activated after the last person to use them has paid their bill. If this hasn't yet happened, the pump's screen will still show the amount of fuel pumped and the price to pay. Wait until those numbers reset to zero, which means the prior customer has paid, at which point you can fill your tank.

*Pro tip:* The cheapest gas is usually at the stations attached to supermarkets, and the most expensive gas is usually at the stations along the *autoroutes* (freeways).

## French Traffic Circles

The British may have invented the traffic circle (aka roundabout) but France has more than any other country—about half of all traffic circles in the world!

So, prepare to go in circles when you are in France. **The key thing to remember:** the cars already in the circle have the right of way, not the car entering it. Don't forget this unless you want to learn all about French tow trucks and how well your car insurance works.

Most traffic circles are small, but some are so large they have more than one lane, for example an inner lane and an outer lane. French drivers, who are used to this, will enter the circle at the outer lane, move to the inner lane as they make their way around the circle, then move back to the outer lane for their exit. However, unless you are used to driving in big traffic circles, I suggest you do what I do and stay in the outer lane. Otherwise, you might have an accident and get to learn about those French tow trucks.

If you are in a traffic circle and you miss your exit, no problem, just go around again. Do not repeat what I once saw a French driver do: stop and back up. *Mon dieu!*

## Narrow French Roads

France, like a lot of European countries, has many roads that are quite narrow. You may find yourself driving on one and see a car approaching from the opposite direction and wonder, "How are we going to avoid hitting each other?" The answer is to slow down, move to the right edge of the road, and pass. You will be surprised how much room there is.

Sometimes a road is so narrow that this won't work. This usually happens in small towns where buildings crowd the road. When this happens, one car will stop at a relatively wide spot in the road and let the other pass.

***Pro tip:*** If you move to the right edge of a country road to let another car pass, be aware that there are lots of irrigation ditches in Provence, right along the edge of the road. Don't go so far right that your tires drop into one!

## French Toll Roads

When you drive long distances in France, you usually take an *autoroute* (aka freeway or motorway.) For these you have to pay a toll, which is based on how far you drive. Here's how these toll roads work.

When you enter the *autoroute*, you'll come to a toll booth that dispenses tickets. You drive up to the dispenser and a ticket will print out next to your window. Take this ticket, and the barrier blocking your lane will go up so you can enter the road. **Don't lose this ticket.**

When you leave the road, you'll come to another toll booth, called a *péage*, where you pay. This is where things get tricky.

Each lane of the *péage* will have a screen above it with a symbol, indicating how to pay. Here's what they look like, plus there are descriptions below.

**An image of a yellow, lower-case letter t** means it's for cars that have an automatic payment device in them, a *télépéage*. If your rental car is equipped with one, you can use these lanes and sail on through. You'll get charged later.

**An image of two white rectangles** on top of each other means you can pay by credit card. You drive up to the barrier that blocks your lane and there will be a machine next to your window. Put your ticket in the slot for tickets and the amount you owe will show on a screen. Press your credit card up to the appropriate spot on the machine for touchless payment, or in the appropriate slot, wait until it's authorized, then remove your card and the barrier will go up. However, **not all foreign cards work**—they must have the right kind of microchip in them (happily, today most cards have the right microchip). If yours doesn't, the machine will reject your card and you will have to back out of this lane, while the cars behind you honk and their drivers shake their fists. It's very dramatic and makes for a memorable vacation moment, just not the good kind.

**An image of cash** means you pay by cash, either inserting money into a machine or tossing coins in a basket. This line is usually long and slow but you may have no choice. The same goes for the line with a cashier (see below.)

**An image of a man** means there is a cashier and you can pay by cash or credit card. This is becoming less common in France as automated machines replace cashiers.

**A green arrow** means you can pay by cash, credit, debit, or *télépéage*.

**A red X** means the lane is closed.

Some lanes have multiple symbols, which means they can be used for any of the things indicated.

While *péages* are at all *autoroute* exits, sometimes they are also found where *autoroutes* come together or split apart. In this case there will be a big *péage* spanning the entire *autoroute* and you'll pay for however far you have gone. Road signs will warn you when you are approaching one of these *péages*, a mile or two ahead of time. A short distance after you leave this *péage* you will come to another one, where you will take a new ticket for the next part of your journey.

## Beware the GPS!

The GPS in your rental car will usually be set properly, but not always. There's a setting called Avoid Toll Roads and **you definitely want it OFF**, otherwise your GPS will never put you on an *autoroute*. It will send you to slower roads instead. Even if you manage to get on an *autoroute*, the GPS will immediately tell you to get off. If you find yourself in this situation, check your car's user manual to see how to fix the setting. Otherwise, you might end up lost in the mountains on a narrow, winding road, as once happened to my nephew when he came to visit.

## Driving in French

The French like to drive much too fast, unless they are driving much too slow. And they love to tailgate so much that you'd think it was the national sport. Plus, they'll stop in the most unusual places—like the middle of an intersection—to look at a map or discuss what to have for lunch.

Ok, I'm exaggerating here, but not by much[*].

---

[*]    tinyurl.com/yd9yry8k

# Dressing

The weather in Provence is mild-to-warm in the spring and autumn, and downright hot in the summer (and sometimes late spring), so dress accordingly. Summer is the time for shorts, skirts, and lightweight tops. And don't forget your bathing suit!

There is occasional rain, and an umbrella can be helpful, but they are hard to pack so I advise buying an inexpensive one when you are here.

As far as style goes, the good people of Provence are not overly concerned with the latest fashion. Sure, they might dress up for a special occasion, and the ladies of Arles in their festival finery are a sight to behold, but casual dress rules the day. Have I ever worn a suit in Provence? Dress shoes? A tie? No, no, and no. So, leave the fancy duds at home.

But do bring a scarf, because it seems like everyone in France wears a scarf. Why are scarves so important? According to Bill Nye the Science Guy, they are not only stylish, but remarkably efficient at keeping you warm[*].

# Biking

Provence is a wonderful place to bike, with many small, quiet roads, plus more and more dedicated bike trails. The availability of electric bikes has exploded in the last few years and many towns have a shop where you

---

[*]     tinyurl.com/y98alzgd

can rent them. I've listed a few of these in this book but more are popping up all the time, so look around or ask at your local tourist office if you need to find one.

# Hiking

France has an excellent system of well-marked and well-maintained hiking trails.

There are three kinds of hiking trails in France. The first are the *sentiers de grande randonee*, denoted by GR followed by a number, like GR7. These are long routes that often connect with those in other countries. Far more numerous are the regional trails, the GRP. And then there are small local trails, the PR.

Hiking routes are periodically identified with yellow arrow signs attached to poles, indicating the distance to a destination (e.g., "Aureilles 6 km"). Along the route, the path will be marked with occasional "blazes" which are colored stripes painted on rocks or trees, indicating the way to go.

The best hiking maps are made by France's national survey agency, the *Institut Géographique National* (IGN.) You can find IGN maps in many newsstands and bookstores. Many tourist offices also have maps of local hikes.

## Look for Local Events

Keep your eyes open for posters announcing upcoming events; you'll usually see them in several locations in a village. They may be for concerts, circuses, village festivals, second hand goods markets (*vide grenier* or *brocante*), etc. You never know when you'll come across a unique local event that isn't on any of the regular tourist websites.

## Taking Your Dog to France

If you are going to be in Provence for a while, you might want to do what we do and bring your faithful pooch. Dogs are welcome almost everywhere, and we take Mica with us when we go to restaurants. One time I even saw a dog racing down the street in a motorcycle sidecar!

Getting your dog into France isn't too hard, but it requires patience and paperwork*, and your canine pal may need to travel in a special compartment under the plane. But it's worth the effort to us dog lovers!

## Some Fun Reading Before You Go

If you'd like to get a sense of Provence before you go, I recommend two terrific authors. Reading them will be like being in Provence before you actually arrive!

The classic Provençal author is Marcel Pagnol. His memoirs *My Father's Glory* and *My Mother's Castle* evoke his childhood in Provence a century ago, while novels like *Jean de Florette* and *Manon of the Spring* tell tales of love and treachery. His books are delightful, by turns touching and funny, and many have been made into movies.

More contemporary is the incomparable Peter Mayle, a Brit who moved to Provence and lived to tell the tale. His books *A Year in Provence* and *Toujours Provence* are full of hilarious insights into the region and its people.

I wouldn't think of putting myself in the same class as these great authors, but I've written two funny books that you might enjoy, *One Sip at a Time* and *Are We French Yet?* about my life in Provence.

---

\*     tinyurl.com/y9llz5r2

# Provençal Culture

## How Many Kisses?

In Provence, as in the rest of France, people often give *les bises*—little kisses on the cheek—when greeting one another. But how many, and which cheek do you start with? **You don't want to get this wrong**—imagine that you go left, he goes right, and you end up kissing on the lips!

Kissing rules vary by region, and even within a region. It's three kisses in western Provence, for example, but changes to two as you move eastward, with no clear border between the two areas. There's an interesting map[*] that's been made, with the results of a nationwide survey—if you hover your cursor over a region, or touch it lightly on a touchpad, you can see the kissing statistics.

---

[*]     tinyurl.com/rtbhxds2

## Provençal Expressions

A friend once complained to me about his drinking buddy, a notorious tightwad. "Whenever it's time to pay the bill," he said, "Gilles has *oursins dans la poche*."

The expression, originally from Marseille, means having sea urchins in your pocket. In other words, you can't reach your wallet!

Provence has a lot of these colorful expressions*. My favorite is for when something is taking too long: you say you have *le temps de tuer un âne à coups de figues* (enough time to kill a donkey by throwing figs at it.) If you consider how tough donkeys are, and how soft figs are, this is a long time indeed.

## The National Sport of Provence

Pétanque, similar to bocce or lawn bowling, is practically a religion in Provence†. People play it in towns large and small, and the annual tournament in Marseille draws over 100,000 spectators.

The game is simple enough that anyone can enjoy it, no matter what their skill level. It doesn't require much equipment, just a flat stretch of ground and a set of metal balls. And it may be the only sport where drinking is encouraged!

---

\*     tinyurl.com/y922dtwc
†     tinyurl.com/2nmzh3nr

# French People are like Coconuts

There's a French expression I hear from time to time: *French people are like coconuts, Americans are like peaches*. The idea is that French people can be hard on the outside, while Americans are much softer.

This can make the French seem aloof and even rude, but if you penetrate that tough exterior, you'll find a very soft center*.

Given these differences, can you actually become friends with a French person? *Oui!* And it's not hard if you know how†.

# Legends of Provence

Provence has a lot of great legends‡. Did you know that Mary Magdalene sailed to Provence from the Holy Land and lived out her days in a local grotto? Or that Saint

---

* tinyurl.com/y9vmlf5g
† tinyurl.com/y9kk9777
‡ tinyurl.com/yyktlo63

Martha subdued a terrible monster that was terrorizing Provence? And let's not forget the sardine that blocked the port of Marseille!

# French Social Life

It is said that French social life revolves around the table, which is to say that the French spend plenty of time together over meals. And while they famously care a lot about food and wine, they aren't snobby about it—a French person hosting a dinner party, for example, will often include store-bought dishes in the menu. The important thing is to spend time together.

It makes me think of what a French friend once told me. "The best wine," he said, "the very best, is the one you share with friends. It doesn't matter what the vintage is, or the name on the label. It's the act of drinking it with friends that makes it great."

# The Animal Kingdom of Provence

Provence is proud of its traditions, many of which involve animals[*]. There's the transhumance, for example, where shepherds guide flocks of sheep through Provençal villages. And the festival of Saint Eloi, where horses get the day off and stroll about with flowers in their manes. For excitement, there are the *abrivados* where French cowboys on horseback corral bulls charging through town. And let's not forget the snail ranchers!

# Christmas in Provence

Provence has some great Christmas traditions[†], like the *gros souper* (big dinner) with its *treize* (yes, 13!) desserts. And the famous santons, those little figurines, began as a way to create nativity scenes when religious displays were banned by the French Revolution.

---

[*]    tinyurl.com/yxsyyu9v
[†]    tinyurl.com/y9whhkmz

# PROVENCE OVERVIEW

# How to Spend a Week in Provence

How should you spend a week in Provence? However you want! But I'll give you some ideas to get you started. Here is an itinerary with a mix of historical sites, hilltop villages, and local markets. If you would like to stay in one spot and make day trips from there, rather than changing hotels frequently, **a good base of operations is St-Rémy-de-Provence**. Everything listed here is within an hour drive of St-Rémy.

One of the glories of Provence is its outdoor markets, and the essential guide is Marjorie Williams' *Markets of Provence*[*]. It's a handy little book with everything you need to enjoy the markets to the fullest.

It is also important to have **a list of market days**, showing which towns have markets on which day. You can find such a list in the Resources section of this book. **Market days are an important consideration**

---

[*]    tinyurl.com/2fjfkvre

in planning your trip, either to visit a particular market or to avoid the crowds that market days bring.

One other piece of advice: **try not to overbook yourself**, because Provence rewards slow travel. Leave time for serendipitous adventures!

# Day 1: Avignon

Avignon was home to the papacy in the 14th century, and the city is dominated by the former papal palace. Take your time visiting this vast and beautiful Palais des Papes, then head to the Couscousserie d'Horloge for lunch. Or buy gourmet goodies at the Les Halles market and picnic on Barthelasse Island—you'll have **an amazing view of Avignon.** After lunch, explore the crooked streets of the *centre ville* and admire its massive ramparts. Walk onto the Saint-Bénézet bridge, known as the Pont d'Avignon in the famous song. Finish with a drink at one of the cafés on the Place de l'Horloge.

# Day 2: Carrières de Lumières and Les Baux-de-Provence

Start your day off with a bang at the immersive sound-and-light show Carrières de Lumières. It is one of the most popular sites in Provence, so **go early** before the parking lots fill up. After the show, walk to Les Baux and its château for the great views, and enjoy the demonstrations of medieval weapons (these are popular with kids, especially the catapult.) Have lunch at Le Clos Saint-Roch restaurant in nearby Maussane-les-Alpilles. In the afternoon, pick up Provençal goodies at the Jean Martin boutique, then sample some of the **world's best olive oil** at Moulin Jean-Marie Cornille or Moulin Castelas. Have a drink on the town's central square, or go straight to the source and taste wine at nearby Mas Sainte-Berthe.

## Day 3: The Luberon Valley

Head to Gordes and stop at the **famous photo spot** on the way into town. From there, don't go directly into Gordes but instead take the turnoff to Sénanque Abbey—you'll avoid crowds if you go early. After that, have a coffee on the terrace at Gordes' Le Cercle Républicain café, with a wonderful view of the Luberon Valley. Now go to Roussillon and enjoy lunch at Restaurant David, looking out on the colorful landscape. After lunch, walk through the vivid ochre quarries on the *Sentier des Ocres* (be sure to dust yourself off when you finish!) Then drive to Café de France in Lacoste and enjoy the view over a glass of rosé.

## Day 4: Arles or Nîmes?

These were both important cities in the Roman Empire, and their attractions are similar, so you might want to visit only one.

**Arles.** Start with the Roman arena, now sparkling clean after a recent scrubbing. Then walk to the Roman theater, which was buried for centuries and only rediscovered in the 19th century. Have lunch at a café on the Place du Forum—one still looks like it did when van Gogh painted it! Explore the Alyscamps Roman burial ground, then head to the Museum of Ancient Arles to see its Roman artifacts, including an ancient barge over 100 feet long. For something more modern, don't miss the funky LUMA tower designed by Frank Gehry, or Villa Benkemoun and its groovy 1970s architecture.

**Nîmes.** Start with the outstanding Roman arena, then admire the nearby Maison Carrée, considered the world's most perfect Roman temple. The Roman history museum across the street is full of interactive displays, including a fun one that lets you "dress like a Roman." Enjoy lunch at the museum's La Table du 2 brasserie, with an outstanding view of the Roman arena. After lunch, take a short walk to see the looming Tour Magne tower, part of the city's ancient fortifications. Then head north to the magnificent Pont du Gard aqueduct. With three levels of arches, it's as tall as the Statue of Liberty's torch!

# Day 5: St-Rémy-de-Provence

Start your day with a coffee at the Grand Café Riche, then take the van Gogh walk through town to see where he painted his masterpieces. Visit his room at the former asylum in Saint-Paul de Mausole, then cross the street to see two massive Roman monuments. Enjoy lunch at Le

Bistro Découverte  on the bustling main road, then try the chocolates at Joël Durand, **the best chocolate shop in Provence**. After lunch, head to Château Romanin for wine tasting, with a stop at the next-door aerodrome to watch the gliders take off and land.

# Day 6: l'Isle-sur-la-Sorgue and Fontaine-de-Vaucluse

l'Isle-sur-la-Sorgue is one of France's **largest antique marketplaces**, with dozens of antique shops and two gigantic fairs a year. Wander through the shops and have a coffee at the Café de France on the central square, then head to lunch. The Sorgue River runs through town, lined with bustling restaurants, so find one that strikes your fancy. My favorite restaurant, though it doesn't have a view, is La Libellule. After lunch, head to Fontaine-de-Vaucluse to see where the Sorgue River is born—it bursts forth from one of the world's largest springs! If you want to finish your day with some exercise, kayak from Fontaine de Vaucluse back to l'Isle-sur-la-Sorgue.

# Day 7: Aix-en-Provence

Start your day with a coffee among the blossoms at Aix's daily flower market, then wander the streets of the city's old town. If you'd like to enjoy some art, the Hotel de Caumont art center and the Musée Granet are both excellent choices. Have lunch at La Fromagerie du Passage, a combination cheese shop and restaurant, and be sure to buy some tasty *fromage* on your way out. Visit Cézanne's old art studio, kept much as he left it, then have a coffee on Cours Mirabeau and enjoy **one of France's best people-watching spot**s. If you love those little santon figurines, be sure to visit one of Provence's top shops, Santons Fouques.

# MY PROVENCE FAVORITES

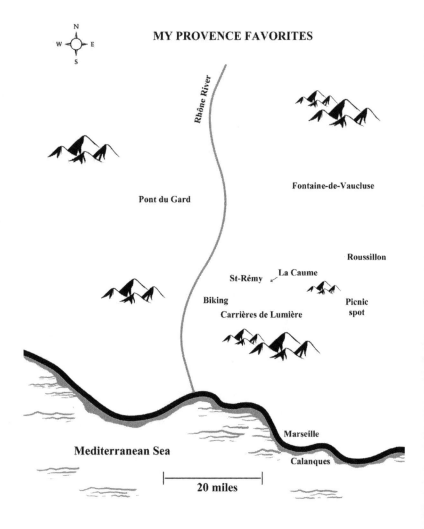

N
W · E
S

Rhône River

Pont du Gard

Fontaine-de-Vaucluse

Roussillon

St-Rémy

La Caume

Biking

Picnic spot

Carrières de Lumière

Mediterranean Sea

Marseille

Calanques

20 miles

# My 10 Favorite Things to Do in Provence

## The Outdoor Markets

One of the glories of Provence is its outdoor markets, full of wonderful sights, smells, and tastes. You can sample cheeses, drool over roast chickens, and chat with the olive vendor. You can get gifts to take home, then have a drink in a café. You can't visit Provence without going to its markets—every town and village has its own. My favorite, of course, is St-Rémy's. (page 63)

## Magic in a Mountain

Imagine this: you enter a giant cavern with sheer, 30-foot-high walls. Huge images start to appear on one wall, then another, then on the floor. You realize that they are paintings by a great artist like van Gogh or Cézanne. The images pulse and swirl, full of life and color, their movements choreographed to beautiful music. This is the Carrières de Lumières, the world's most magical sound and light show, and a different artist is featured each year. It's so popular that copies are popping up all over the world, but none matches the original; you really do have to see it to believe it. (page 89)

# France's Fjords

East of Marseille, tall cliffs plunge down to the sea, with craggy inlets here and there. These calanques are like mini-fjords, their grey stone walls contrasting with the deep blue waters of the Mediterranean. You can see sailboats anchored in them, their passengers sunning on tiny beaches. If you are feeling energetic you can hike to the calanques, but I recommend taking one of the regular boat rides that depart from the pretty little port town of Cassis—you can see the calanques in two hours or less. Be sure to enjoy some seafood at one of the restaurants along Cassis's waterfront. (page 171)

# Walk Through a Rainbow

A century ago, ochre was mined in Roussillon and used as pigment in paint. The ochre quarries are abandoned now but there's a well-marked walking trail through them. Follow it and admire the brilliantly-colored hillsides—you'll see red, purple, orange, and yellow. The town of Roussillon is a nice place to enjoy lunch or coffee, and all the buildings are painted in various ochre shades. Nearby and less crowded is the Colorado

Provençal, with its own abandoned ochre quarries, and the Bruoux ochre mines, a labyrinth of brightly-colored tunnels 30 feet high. (page 143)

## The Stunning Roman Aqueduct

The Pont du Gard was built over 2,000 years ago, to bring water to the city of Nîmes. It is so tall that the Roman engineers had to build it in three levels, each with its own set of arches. The aqueduct crosses over the Gard River and is nearly 200 feet high! For extra fun you can rent a kayak and float under it. (page 185)

## Hike to the Top of the World

La Caume is one of the highest points of the Alpilles Mountains and is surprisingly easy to reach on foot. Rather than starting at the bottom, you can drive to a big parking lot that's part of the way up and join the trail there. It's paved and well-marked and not too steep, and the view from La Caume is terrific—to the north you can see the Rhône Valley and to the south the view goes all the way to the Mediterranean Sea. (page 118)

## A River of Sheep

Every year, thousands of sheep march through the streets of St-Rémy, accompanied by musicians, shepherds, sheepdogs, and the occasional goat. It's like a river of sheep flowing through town! Afterwards there are sheepdog trials. This is a fun event for the whole family. It's all part of an annual festival that commemorates the days when sheep used to walk to higher pastures to escape the summer heat. (page 71)

## Picnic in the Sky

The Cedar Forest sits far above the Luberon Valley, higher even than the nearby hilltop village of Bonnieux. As you take the winding road up to the forest, there's a secret spot off to the side where you can picnic under a tree and enjoy an unparalleled view. (page 145)

## Birth of a River

Imagine that you are walking upstream on a path next to a river. You look up and see that you are coming to a high cliff. You wonder how the river gets past it— maybe it goes around? Then you get to the cliff and you realize the river is coming *out of the ground*, just bursting forth. You're at Fontaine-de-Vaucluse, one of the largest springs in the world, and so deep that even the famous undersea explorer Jacques Cousteau couldn't reach the bottom. (page 138)

# Bike to Hell and Back

The Alpilles Mountains are full of biking routes with fabulous views, that range from easy to moderately difficult. Our favorite ride is to puff our way up to the Val d'Enfer (Hell Valley.) It's full of rugged boulders and rocky outcroppings and there's a spot where you can look straight across to the mountaintop fortress of Les Baux-de-Provence. The best part of the ride is coasting back! (page 124)

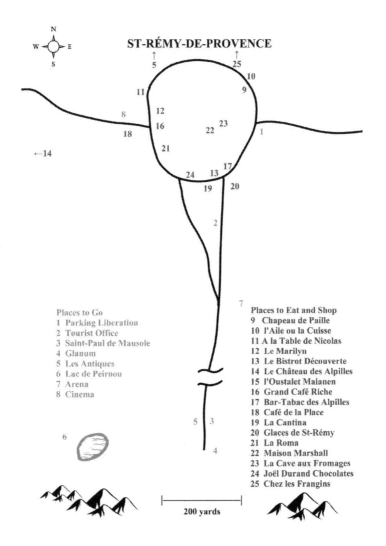

# ST-RÉMY-DE-PROVENCE

**Places to Go**
1 Parking Liberation
2 Tourist Office
3 Saint-Paul de Mausole
4 Glanum
5 Les Antiques
6 Lac de Peiroou
7 Arena
8 Cinema

**Places to Eat and Shop**
9 Chapeau de Paille
10 l'Aile ou la Cuisse
11 A la Table de Nicolas
12 Le Marilyn
13 Le Bistrot Découverte
14 Le Château des Alpilles
15 l'Oustalet Maianen
16 Grand Café Riche
17 Bar-Tabac des Alpilles
18 Café de la Place
19 La Cantina
20 Glaces de St-Rémy
21 La Roma
22 Maison Marshall
23 La Cave aux Fromages
24 Joël Durand Chocolates
25 Chez les Frangins

200 yards

# St-Rémy-de-Provence

## Introduction

Val and I live part of the year in St-Rémy, and because we know the area so well, I've devoted a section of this book to St-Rémy and another section to the towns nearby.

We fell in love with St-Rémy the first time we visited, nearly 30 years ago. We tried living in other towns in Provence but kept coming back to this one. It's the perfect size for us, big enough to have plenty of shops and cafés, but small enough that we can walk from the middle of town to the countryside in a few minutes. And it has the best outdoor market in Provence.

St-Rémy sits next to the Alpilles Mountains, a great area for hiking and biking. The town began as the Gallo-Roman settlement of Glanum, and you can visit its ruins at the foot of the Alpilles. Across the street are some impressive Roman monuments.

St-Rémy's best-known resident was Vincent van Gogh, who spent a year in the local mental asylum. You can see his old room, kept just as it was when he lived there. Posters of van Gogh's works are placed around town at the spots where he painted them, and it's fascinating to compare his paintings with the real thing—they help you understand his unique artistic vision.

St-Rémy's other famous resident was the medieval seer Nostradamus, known for his cryptic prophesies. He was born and raised in St-Rémy before moving to another town nearby.

The tourist office[*] is at Place Jean Jaurès[†]. A private group has created a detailed map of the central city[‡] that is very helpful.

## Highlights

- *You can see the places where Vincent **van Gogh painted his masterpieces**, and visit the asylum where he lived*

- *St-Rémy has one of the **best outdoor markets** in Provence*

- *In the spring, **thousands of sheep march through the streets** during the annual transhumance festival*

- *The ancient city of Glanum sits above St-Rémy and **the view from it is spectacular***

---

[*]   tinyurl.com/5tmzwd4x

[†]   tinyurl.com/yv3uh3v4

[‡]   tinyurl.com/u8fvkdt5

- *On a sunny day, you can enjoy a **picnic at a secret lake***

- *St-Rémy's Master Chocolatier makes some of the **best chocolates in France***

- *There is a **hidden parking lot** that only the locals know about (shh, I'll tell you how to find it)*

- *Don't miss **my favorite restaurants and cafés***

## Vincent van Gogh in St-Rémy

Vincent van Gogh spent several years in Provence, first in Arles and then—after that unfortunate business with his ear—in a mental asylum in St-Rémy called Saint-Paul de Mausole[*][†].

A former Franciscan monastery, Saint-Paul de Mausole provided a peaceful setting for van Gogh to calm his troubled mind. He spent a year there, producing over 100 paintings, including masterpieces like *The Starry Night* and *Irises*.

Van Gogh had a small room on the second floor of the asylum and it is still kept **the same way it was** when he lived there. I like to look out his window and wonder: What was he thinking?

The grounds of Saint-Paul de Mausole are beautiful, especially the garden, and you should **take a few minutes**

---

[*]    tinyurl.com/ypt2vtmw
[†]    tinyurl.com/ve35fpan

**to look around**. You'll find reproductions of some of van Gogh's paintings, placed in the same spots where he painted them. You can **compare what things really look like** with how he painted them, and they are often very different.

To see reproductions of other van Gogh paintings, in the spots where he painted them, there's an excellent self-guided walk in St-Rémy, with an inexpensive audio guide—ask at the tourist office* for information.

Across the street from Saint-Paul de Mausole are *les Antiques*, two giant Roman monuments that only take a few minutes to see. You should definitely walk over and check them out. If you have time, you can also visit the ruins of the ancient Roman city of Glanum, which is right next door.

---

*    tinyurl.com/yv3uh3v4    🌐

# The Best Outdoor Market

If you love outdoor markets, **don't miss St-Rémy's**. It has everything you want in a Provençal market, from fruits and vegetables to olives and cheeses to colorful crafts. It starts early on Wednesday morning and finishes around noon, and you should **go early** because the market gets crowded. There's another market on Saturday morning but it's very small.

The market is spread all over town and has **three main sections**—in front of the church, in the main square, and in the parking lot across from the church.

I suggest starting in front of the church* because it's easy to find. If you get there early, you'll see the **paëlla**

---

* tinyurl.com/3duernvr

**man** stirring his steaming paëlla in a big round pan nearly three feet across. Paëlla is a Spanish dish made of seasoned rice with seafood, chorizo and sometimes chicken, and is popular in Provençal markets. The locals line up to get some for lunch and it's really good—try it!

Nearby is a boulangerie and a place to get newspapers (both to the left as you face the church), plus a stand that specializes in fruits. I love seeing how the fruit changes with the seasons, starting with strawberries in the spring, then later cherries, and in the summer it's stone fruits and melons.

If you feel like having a coffee and a croissant to start your day, one of my favorite spots is the Grand Café Riche[*] to the right of the church as you face it[†]. It's got a very old-timey look, like something out of Paris in the 1800s.

When you are ready to move on, Rue Lafayette will take you to the center of town and the heart of the market. Along the way you'll pass a vendor selling honey and another selling jam—I like to take little jars of honey home as gifts. There's usually someone selling sachets of lavender, another nice gift. One vendor sells cans of *foie gras* and *confit de canard* (duck leg confit), two French specialties I love.

Rue Lafayette ends at the town's main square, Place Jules Pelissier[‡] in front of the mayor's office. **My favorite olive vendor** is there, with more than a dozen kinds of

---

[*]    tinyurl.com/4vraj2c5
[†]    tinyurl.com/pnwka7mm 🌐
[‡]    tinyurl.com/4ymxrmpr 🌐

olives. He also has spreads like tapenade (made from olives and anchovies), pistounade (olives and basil), and caviar d'aubergine (eggplant)—tasty things to put on bread or crackers at aperitif time. Try some! Pick out what you want and the vendor will fill up a container until you tell him to stop.

Nearby is a **big rotisserie with chickens turning on the spit**. If you don't see it, just follow your nose. There's nothing better than a hot and juicy roast chicken, especially a French one. And the potatoes! They roast them at the bottom of the rotisserie with chicken fat dripping on them. Totally decadent. Chicken and potatoes are great for a casual lunch, but be sure to have plenty of napkins.

The **cheese lady** is near the chicken man, with lots and lots of cheeses. Sample a few! Charles de Gaulle once complained about the fractious French by asking, "How do you govern a country with 246 kinds of cheese?" There is also a vendor selling sliced ham and another selling sausages and salamis.

You'll find more vendors in some of the streets that radiate out from the square, and still more on the ring road that encircles the central part of St-Rémy. The ring road is where you will find many of the crafts and jewelry you are looking for. If you follow the Rue de la Commune from the square out to the ring road, just a few steps to your left is another one of my favorite places for a coffee, the Bar-Tabac des Alpilles[*] at 21 Boulevard

---

[*]    tinyurl.com/nbkcjxts

Victor Hugo*. It's also a good place for lunch or dinner or an afternoon drink.

Head back to the church and look across the street to find the third main section of the market, held in the town's central parking lot† (**see the section just below on Parking** to learn where to park.) There's a **carousel** in one corner, which is great for young kids. This part of the market has clothing, colorful tablecloths, kitchenware, lavender, and more. There's also a small *brocante* (flea market) with fun items from the old days—you can wander through it to find a memento to take home.

At the back of the parking lot is another favorite spot for a coffee, the Café de la Place‡§. The food is excellent if you'd like to eat there—take a look at their chalkboard to see what's on the menu.

Later in the morning, a small musical group sets up at the intersection in front of the church. Grab a seat at any of the cafés lining the road to enjoy the music.

If you'd like to have lunch after your visit to the market, check out the Restaurants section for ideas on where to eat. But be sure to **make a reservation** or arrive early because they fill up fast on market days.

---

\*   tinyurl.com/df5x3nnn

†   tinyurl.com/2be4pwkc

‡   tinyurl.com/spmjax8s

§   tinyurl.com/8rkx9she

# The Hidden Parking Lot

Parking in town is limited, with a small parking lot across from the church and another near the tourist office, while on-street parking fills up quickly. Very frustrating! But I'm here to tell you about **a hidden parking lot that always has space and is free of charge**, but can be tricky to find. It's so well hidden that I lived in St-Rémy for years before I found it. Now it's the only place I park.

It's called **Parking de la Libération**[*] on Avenue de la Libération, near the intersection with Boulevard Mirabeau. It is not well marked and even a GPS has a hard time finding it, but the description below will lead you to it. There is also an article[†] I suggest you read because it includes helpful photos.

If you are arriving from out of town, you will probably find yourself on the D99 at some point. This is the main east-west road between Cavaillon and Tarascon. Get off the D99 onto the D99A on the *East* side of town (there are two such intersections.) Go a mile, until just BEFORE you dead end onto Boulevard Mirabeau— you'll see the dead-end directly ahead. On your left will be something that looks like extra space between buildings but is actually a driveway. **That's the entrance to the parking lot.** There's a small sign pointing left, marked Parking de la Libération, but it's easy to miss.

---

[*]   tinyurl.com/4d6azasn
[†]   tinyurl.com/y78nfkyl

Alternatively, if you are already in St.-Rémy, you will probably be on the ring road that circles the center part of town. It changes names several times and at one point becomes Boulevard Mirabeau. When you get to this section, stay in the right lane and take the exit towards Cavaillon (there is a sign pointing towards the right.) About 70 yards after you take this exit, at the crosswalk, the parking lot entry will be on your right. **Go slow or you'll miss it!**

As you enter the parking lot (really a series of lots), you will first hit a small parking lot that is always full. Don't worry, continue to the far end of the lot and follow the *SORTIE* (exit) sign.

Now you will be in a larger parking lot that is also probably full. Drive out the exit on the far side (that is, to the right as you first enter the parking lot.) As you drive through this parking lot, **keep your eye out** for a sign on your right that says *CENTRE VILLE*—this is the walking path you'll take into town.

As you exit this second parking lot, going up a little ramp, you will enter a third parking lot that looks like the second one. It is often full, especially on market days. Never fear! Keep going, out the far side of this lot and up another ramp.

Now you've hit the fourth lot, which is really just a large field, but it has plenty of parking. I've seen it get crowded but never full. You should be able to park here.

Now go back to the walking path into town, the one marked *CENTRE VILLE*. Nearby are some public toilets, which could come in handy.

When you get into town **be sure to note where you are** so you can find your way back later. As a reminder, the path is on Rue Marius Jouveau.*

When you go back to your car, **don't try to exit the way you entered**, as this is a "one way" parking lot. Instead, continue on the dirt road in the parking lot to the far side and go out that way.

## Roman Sites

At the southern edge of St-Rémy are two Roman sites, Glanum[†][‡] and *les Antiques*[§]. You can combine a visit to one or both with a visit to Saint-Paul de Mausole, where Vincent van Gogh spent a year in an asylum. The three sites are all **within short walking distance** of one another.

Glanum was originally a Celtic settlement, at the foot of the Alpilles mountains and near a sacred spring. After the Roman conquest, it became an important cultural center, with grand temples and public baths and a central forum. The city was eventually abandoned and

---

\*    tinyurl.com/4r8j4hku  

†    tinyurl.com/sn7vhbtk

‡    tinyurl.com/au8ye8uk   🌐

§    tinyurl.com/b8fub4a   🌐

fell into disrepair, and some of its stones were hauled away and used for construction in St-Rémy.

Glanum was much smaller than other nearby Roman cities like Arles and Nîmes, so if you want a taste of Roman history but don't want to spend a lot of time, this is a good choice. The site is well-marked and there is a nice museum next to it, so it's also good for those with a deeper interest. If you go, be sure to **climb up to the highest point** for panoramic views over St-Rémy and the Rhône Valley.

Right next to Glanum are two large Roman monuments called *les Antiques*. One is a mausoleum and the other is the oldest triumphal arch in France, kind of like the Arc de Triomphe in Paris but smaller. It only takes a few minutes to walk around and enjoy what's carved on them (see if you can find the character that looks like a space alien.)

# The Transhumance Festival

Provence has a lot of sheep, *a lot.* You can see flocks of them in the countryside, with a shepherd standing nearby and sheepdogs alert for danger. There's an aerodrome near St-Rémy where gliders take off and land in a big, grassy field, and sheep come in a few times a year to "mow" the lawn.

Provence gets hot in the summer, so the sheep head to cooler mountain pastures. They used to go by foot, marching through village after village, in a procession called the transhumance. This was a big deal and everyone would come out to watch it.

Eventually, shepherds started transporting their flocks by truck and the transhumance died out. But the tradition was revived in the 1980s with transhumance festivals, and St-Rémy has one of the best. It's held every year in late May or early June and you shouldn't miss it.

During the festival, **thousands of sheep march through town**, baaing all the way. Bands play as they go around the town's ring road, accompanied by shepherds, sheepdogs, and the occasional goat. It's like **a river of sheep**!

Crowds line the road, taking pictures and reaching out to stroke the sheep as they go by. One year it was unseasonably cool and I could feel the heat rising off the flocks. The ring road is long enough that it's easy to find a front row seat. This is a fun event for the whole family.

St-Rémy has put together a great video[*] of the transhumance (short) if you'd like to get an idea of what it's like.

The transhumance takes place in the morning, and in the afternoon there are sheepdog trials north of town. If you plan to have lunch, be sure to **make a reservation** or come early because restaurants fill up fast.

*Pro tip:* if you walk in the street after thousands of sheep have gone by, be sure to watch where you step!

## A Secret Picnic Spot

About two miles from the center of St-Rémy[†] is a shady picnic spot known only to the locals[‡]. It sits along the

---

[*]    tinyurl.com/yvvva6w6

[†]    tinyurl.com/apbdtwj9

[‡]    tinyurl.com/yajavf73

shore of a lake created thousands of years ago by the Romans, and is a nice place to get away from the crowds for a few hours.

Lac du Peiroou is a small reservoir, created by a dam that spans a narrow gap between two rocky outcroppings. While the current dam was built a century ago, the original dates back to the first century B.C., when the Romans built it to supply water to Glanum.

The lake has a **wide, grassy area** at one end, with trees that provide welcome shade on a sunny Provençal day. It's the perfect place to spread out a blanket and enjoy a lazy afternoon. You can stock up for your picnic at St-Rémy's weekly market, or try the Jardin des Alpilles[*][†]. It's my go-to spot for all picnic supplies, including wine.

You can splash around in the lake to cool off, but don't try catching any fish – you need a special permit for that. And there are trails around the lake and into the hills if you want to stretch your legs. Or you can just relax, read a book and think about where you are going to have dinner.

To get to the lake, head south out of St.-Rémy. About half a mile past the Tourist Office, make a right turn onto Avenue Antoine de la Salle. There's a small sign marking the route to Lac du Peiroou but go slowly and look carefully because it's easy to miss.

---

[*]    tinyurl.com/m6bdech
[†]    tinyurl.com/wsdbs55v

After about a quarter mile, the road will fork and there won't be any signs telling you which way to go. Take the left fork and continue about a mile. At this point there will be a little road leading off to the left and you'll see a small parking lot, with the lake next to it.

If you drive, be careful along the last stretch because the road is narrow and twisty. You can bike or walk to the lake but beware – there are some steep stretches that you will want to avoid on a hot day.

## Young Men in Tight White Pants

Every region of France has its own customs, and one of the things unique to Provence is its connection to bulls, which is evident in the cuisine, the festivals and the local sports.

One way the young men of Provence demonstrate their bravery is in the *course camarguaise*\*, what some people call French bull fighting. But it's not fighting at all and the bulls don't get hurt. Instead, little doodads are tied

---

\*    tinyurl.com/y9fmu65w

around their horns and the young men, the *rasateurs*, have to run up to the bulls and take off the doodads. It's a popular event, filling arenas throughout Provence. Some of the bulls become so famous that they have endorsement contracts!

Val loves the sport because the *rasateurs* wear white shirts and pants, fitted very snugly. She calls them "the young men in their tight white pants."

A *course* is exciting, with *rasateurs* running up to a bull and then the bull chasing the *rasateurs*, who escape by leaping over fences. Remarkably, I've been to many *courses* and have seen a young man get hurt only once, and even then it wasn't bad (he bumped his knee on the fence.)

A *course* is sometimes preceded by an *abrivado*, an exciting event in itself. Bulls are run one by one through the streets of town, ending up at the arena. They are led by *gardians* (French cowboys, both women and men) that guide them with their horses. It's a display of horsemanship that only the best *gardians* can master. It usually go off without a hitch but once I saw a bull get away and go rampaging down the street. Luckily, spectators stand safely behind metal barriers.

St-Rémy has an arena for the *course camaguaise*, the Arénes Municipal Coinon[*]. A number of other nearby towns also have arenas, like Chateaurenard and Mouriès. Check at the tourist office for the schedule if you'd like to experience this unique Provence tradition. The biggest

---

[*]   tinyurl.com/rzxsd4c

and most elaborate *courses* are in the Roman arena in Arles, especially the ones that take place on Easter weekend and the first Monday of July.

# A Cool Walk on a Hot Day

The area around St-Rémy is wonderful for hiking. The Alpilles Mountains are crisscrossed with well-marked trails that offer fabulous views. But on a hot day, you might want a cooler way to stretch your legs. So, do what the locals do and take a canal walk*.

St-Rémy is in an agricultural area with a vast network of irrigation canals, built around the main *Canal des Alpines*. This canal and its offshoots are like a bunch of little rivers with **shady walking paths** alongside them.

My favorite starting point is at **the waterfall**† next the D99A road as it enters St-Rémy from the east. Tourists like to stop here to take a photo—there's a small area just across the road where you can park. If you follow the canal upstream about 100 yards you will come to a split. You can follow the path to the left and go a long way, with **great views** of vineyards and the Alpilles beyond. You'll often find townspeople there, walking their dogs.

If instead you go to the right, you'll amble towards town, passing *bassins* full of croaking frogs, with the occasional peep into someone's back yard.

---

\*　tinyurl.com/3rw644j2

†　tinyurl.com/3fxw5xe4

Alternatively, you can follow the canal downstream from the waterfall, where you'll soon cross over the main road—what looks like a normal overpass is actually an elevated canal! Continue for a mile or so and you will be rewarded with **beautiful views of St-Rémy.**

The network of canals extends far beyond St-Rémy, towards Eygalières in the east, St.-Ètienne-du-Grès in the west and Maillane in the north. Check Google Maps to trace their path and find a spot to begin your walk. It's an unbeatable way to get some cool exercise on a hot day.

## Going to the Movies

Let's say you are expecting beautiful weather, only to discover that it's raining buckets. Or maybe it's one of those days that is so hot you can't move. What to do? Here's an idea—go to the movies[*]!

Yes, there's a nice movie theatre in St-Rémy, the Cinéma Ciné-Palace[†], at 4 avenue Fauconnet[‡] near the town's main parking lot. The theatre is dry and cozy for those rainy days, and cool and refreshing for when it's scorching outside. The seats are comfortable and it's small enough that you can get a good view from any of them.

If you want to know what's showing, you can either drop by the cinema or check its website. If you don't

---

[*]    tinyurl.com/y4ygsv45
[†]    tinyurl.com/2kcdcuva
[‡]    tinyurl.com/s8kp3f7z

speak French, fear not: a lot of films come from English-speaking countries and are shown in their native tongue. **Just look for the letters VO (*version originale*)** on the movie schedule.

If you'd like to go to a movie in another town, nearby Cavaillon has two theatres, the Cinéma La Cigale and the Cinéma Femina and even the little village of Noves has one, the Cinéma l'Eden. If you want to go further afield, there are several options in Avignon.

Of course, it's best to have perfect weather so you can enjoy the beauty of Provence. But sometimes Mother Nature doesn't cooperate and it's good to have alternatives!

# My Favorite Places to Eat

*Pro tip:* cafés and restaurants fill up quickly during tourist season, especially on Wednesday (market day), so be sure to make a reservation or get there early.

### Restaurants

**Le Bistro Découverte**[*]

19 Boulevard Victor Hugo[†]
Tel: +33 (0)4 90 92 34 49

---

[*]   tinyurl.com/2s4ksb62
[†]   tinyurl.com/hrdcjp2a

Le Bistrot Découverte is a restaurant where everything is good. Located near the tourist office, you can eat indoors or out. Be sure to ask about the **wine cellar downstairs** if you'd like to buy a bottle to drink or take with you—you can enter via the restaurant or through a separate entrance on Rue de la Commune.

### À la Table de Nicolas[*]

8 boulevard Marceau[†]
Tel: +33 (0)4 32 62 03 82

Diners at À la Table de Nicolas can take comfort in knowing that Chef Nicolas **understands food allergies**[‡]. His daughter is gluten-intolerant and he's happy to adapt dishes to make them safe for his customers to eat. All his fruits and vegetables are organic and he offers a nice selection of **vegetarian dishes.** And he does all this while earning the title of *Master Restauranteur*! À La Table de Nicolas also offers **a wide variety of takeout dishes.**

### Le Marilyn[§]

13 boulevard Marceau[¶]
Tel: +33 (0)4 90 92 37 11

---

[*]    tinyurl.com/zjbnnku3
[†]    tinyurl.com/eb3ktn7s
[‡]    tinyurl.com/yxwx4fvn
[§]    tinyurl.com/3epxcxtz
[¶]    tinyurl.com/yyhb946v

Le Marilyn is across the street from À la Table de Nicolas. It has a **small menu that changes frequently**, ensuring that everything is **fresh and seasonal**. It's a comfortable place with a friendly staff and is usually one of the first places I check when eating out. And yes, the owner is very blond and looks a bit like you know who.

### L'Aile ou la Cuisse*

34 Boulevard Mirabeau†
Tel: +33 (0)6 12 13 40 40

Want to pick out your own dessert? Try L'Aile ou la Cuisse‡! The menu is traditional but not stuffy and there are plenty of good things to eat—try the farm egg with bacon and mushrooms followed by braised lamb shoulder. **The best part is dessert**—your server will lead you up to a big display case and let you choose your favorite. I like to watch people pick out their dessert and then walk back to their table with gleeful smiles on their faces. It makes them look like kids who just got the best Christmas presents ever.

### Chapeau de Paille§

29 Boulevard Mirabeau¶
Tel: +33 (0)4 90 92 85 78

---

This local favorite has garnered a nice mention in the famous Michelin guide. Its seasonal menu gives pride of place to **Provençal classics** like slow-cooked lamb and Camargue bull, and it's my go-to place for *soupe de pistou* and *le grand aïoli*. Combined with a nice selection of wines by the glass, it's hard to go wrong here.

### Chez les Frangins*

Avenue du 19 mars 1962†
Tel: +33 (0)9 75 77 65 14

Chez les Frangins is an **artisanal rotisserie** with everything you need for a delicious dinner at home, or a picnic under a shady tree. It offers roast chickens, pork spare ribs, legs of lamb, sausages, and more. Add to that a selection of roast potatoes, multiple side dishes, desserts, and drinks, and you may find yourself coming here more than once.

### Le Château des Alpilles‡

1392 Route de Rougadou§
Tel: +33 (0)4 90 92 03 33

Le Château des Alpilles is the place to go for a **special meal**. It's a 5-star hotel and restaurant that you enter via a **majestic avenue lined with plane trees**. The hotel is an elegant old Provençal estate and the food is excellent, but

---

*   tinyurl.com/22dab7dy
†   tinyurl.com/2ykwp22m
‡   tinyurl.com/8vbz725w
§   tinyurl.com/3vz9kcrd

the best part of dining there is sitting outside, surrounded by the park-like grounds. The restaurant gives first choice to hotel guests, who can decide the night before whether they want a table, so it is hard to reserve ahead. The secret is to **call early in the morning** on the day you'd like to dine, at which point you can snag one of the few free tables. It is generally easier to get a reservation for lunch than for dinner.

### L'Oustalet Maianen[*]

16 Avenue Lamartine, Maillane[†]
Tel: +33 (0)4 90 95 74 60

If you'd like a quiet spot not far from of St-Rémy, head north three miles to L'Oustalet Maianen[‡]. It's in the town of Maillaine, where the famous poet Frédéric Mistral lived (there's a small museum about him near the restaurant.) The food is always excellent, as is the service. The owner learned to cook from his father, who ran the restaurant before him, and grew up in the apartment upstairs. This is **definitely worth the short drive.**

## Cafés

If you want to have a coffee and a croissant to start your day, a good spot is the Grand Café Riche[§] at 27

---

[*]  tinyurl.com/5fxxzmv3
[†]  tinyurl.com/vacxmys2 🌐
[‡]  tinyurl.com/bde9xean
[§]  tinyurl.com/4vraj2c5

Boulevard Marceau[*] next to the church….Another good place for a coffee is Bar-Tabac des Alpilles[†] at 21 Boulevard Victor Hugo[‡]. It's also nice for lunch or dinner and it's my favorite spot for an afternoon drink…Café de la Place[§], at 17 Place de la République[⸶] (in the back of the parking lot across from the church), is a good coffee spot with excellent food.

## Pizza / Ice Cream / Pastries / Cheese

La Cantina[**], at 18 Boulevard Victor Hugo[††] has excellent pizza and pasta and real Italian espresso…A popular place for ice cream cones and scoops is Glacés de Saint Rémy at 28 Boulevard Victor Hugo[‡‡] while you'll find fancy ice cream dishes at Le Roma[§§] at 33 Boulevard Marceau[⸶⸶] near the church…At 2 Place Joseph Hilaire[***] is Maison Marshall, with award-winning pastries, and only steps away is St-Rémy's best cheese shop, La Cave aux Fromages[†††], at 1 Place Joseph Hilaire[‡‡‡].

---

[*]     tinyurl.com/pnwka7mm ⊕
[†]     tinyurl.com/nbkcjxts
[‡]     tinyurl.com/df5x3nnn ⊕
[§]     tinyurl.com/spmjax8s
[⸶]     tinyurl.com/8rkx9she ⊕
[**]    tinyurl.com/7rfysv3k
[††]    tinyurl.com/4x6yxa9k ⊕
[‡‡]    tinyurl.com/39w45sp4 ⊕
[§§]    tinyurl.com/uc5enprb
[⸶⸶]    tinyurl.com/yh58dryj ⊕
[***]   tinyurl.com/38m6pm3r ⊕
[†††]   tinyurl.com/6ssfdnuz
[‡‡‡]   tinyurl.com/636cu3ka ⊕

## Chocolate!

St-Rémy is lucky to have its own Master Chocolatier[*], Joël Durand[†], and people come from all over to visit his shop at 3 Boulevard Victor Hugo[‡]. Be sure to **sample his Alphabet of Flavors**—chocolates stamped with different letters of the alphabet. Each has a unique flavor, like chocolate with rosemary or chocolate with lavender (my favorite is chocolate with lime—so good!) Buy some for your friends and spell out a message!

---

[*]    tinyurl.com/f3e5r5s
[†]    tinyurl.com/368ndz6f
[‡]    tinyurl.com/phyb95d8

# NEAR ST-RÉMY-DE-PROVENCE

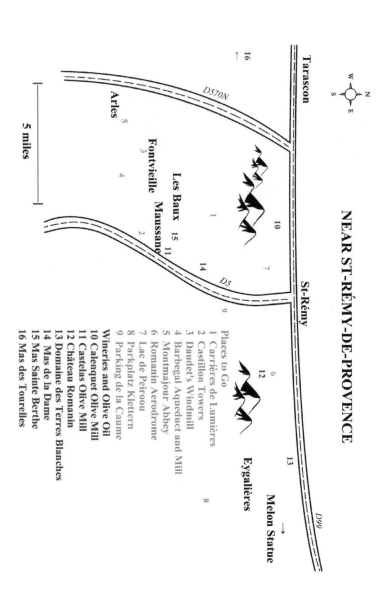

Tarascon

St-Rémy

Eygalières

Melon Statue →

D570N

D5

D99

Arles

Fontvieille

Les Baux

Maussane

16 ←

5 miles

## Places to Go

1 Carrières de Lumières
2 Castillon Towers
3 Daudet's Windmill
4 Barbegal Aqueduct and Mill
5 Montmajour Abbey
6 Romanin Aerodrome
7 Lac de Peirou
8 Parkplatz Klettern
9 Parking de la Caume

## Wineries and Olive Oil

10 Calenquet Olive Mill
11 Castelas Olive Mill
12 Château Romanin
13 Domaine des Terres Blanches
14 Mas de la Dame
15 Mas Sainte Berthe
16 Mas des Tourelles

86

# Near St-Rémy-de-Provence

There are so many interesting sights within 30 minutes of St-Rémy that I created this section just for them. They make for easy day trips from St-Rémy if you are staying there.

The area around St-Rémy isn't dominated by a single town, but instead has lots of little towns and villages that practically beg you to visit.

## Highlights

- *Carrières de Lumières is a magical, immersive sound-and-light show in a giant cavern. **Not to be missed!***

- *The ruined fortress of Les Baux-des-Provence **towers over the surrounding countryside** and the views from it are amazing*

- *Some of the **world's best olive oil** is produced here, and I'll tell you where to taste and buy it*

- *The Alpilles Mountains are crisscrossed with hiking trails and bike routes that offer **fantastic views** (and are not too strenuous.) I share some of my favorites.*

- *You can **soar through the sky** in a glider, or watch the gliders take off and land, at a local airport*

- *The area is full of wineries making **delicious wine** and I point you to some of the best*

- *Don't miss **my favorite restaurants and cafés***

# South of St-Rémy

## Carrières de Lumières (do not miss this!)

Long ago, when stone was needed to build fortresses and châteaux, the best in Provence was found in the Val d'Enfer (Hell Valley.) It was removed in big slabs and you can still see flat rockfaces where it was cut away.

The biggest quarry was inside a mountain, and as stone was removed it created huge rectangular caverns with high walls. These were eventually abandoned and remained cold and dark until someone had a very bright idea. Starting in the 1970s, the caverns became a place for sound-and-light shows, the Carrières de Lumières[*] (Quarries of Light.) It's within walking distance[†] of Les Baux-de-Provence. A new artist is featured every year, like Chagall, Picasso, or Klimt. The shows are very popular so

---

[*]   tinyurl.com/5csr842p
[†]   tinyurl.com/4s586x4p

**be sure to buy your tickets ahead of time**. You should also **try to go early** because the parking can fill up.

What's it like to visit? Let's imagine you walk into the Vincent van Gogh show right before it starts. The cavern is grey and dim and surprisingly cool (bring a sweater.) You notice the flat walls, over 30 feet high, but so far nothing is all that impressive.

Then the lights go out, plunging you into darkness. Images start to appear on the walls—one, two, then a dozen. You see irises here, sunflowers there. A painting of a wheat field starts moving, the shafts of wheat swaying like there's a breeze. It's hard to know where to look, with images on this wall and that wall, even on the floor.

And the music! A classical piece plays, coordinated with the movement of the images. You are surrounded by color, immersed in art and music, and begin to see van Gogh's paintings in a new way, alive and magical.

The show runs continuously, alternating with another short feature, so don't worry if you miss the start of a show—just stay until it cycles back to the point where you began.

I hate to say **you have to be there** but you really do, because it's hard to do the Carrières justice with mere words, but a video* can help.

The show is a technical marvel, with hundreds of high-definition projectors and computers using special effects

---

\*    tinyurl.com/y7cdr5jn

technology to create and coordinate thousands of images. It has been replicated in cities around the world, plus there is a traveling version, but for me the best place is where it began, in a cavern inside a mountain.

## Les Baux-de-Provence and its Fortress

Sitting on top of a giant rock is the medieval fortress of Les Baux-de-Provence*, lord of all it surveys. Driving towards Les Baux, you look up at its sheer stone face and think, "Who would be dumb enough to attack this place?"

Les Baux is the largest of the châteaux (castles) of the Alpilles—the mountains are dotted with them because this has been a strategic location since Roman times. The châteaux are in ruins today because they used to be hotbeds of rebellion, and finally the French king decided to put an end to this nonsense and destroyed them all (some heads rolled in the process.) The history of these châteaux is very interesting, and many can be visited[†].

Below Les Baux's château is the village itself, perched partway up the rock. It's not very big—real estate is tight here—and only a few hundred people live there. But it's still earned its place among *The Most Beautiful Villages of France*[‡] and is definitely worth a look around.

---

[*]     tinyurl.com/4v3774p9
[†]     tinyurl.com/y22ykrmv
[‡]     tinyurl.com/a6ujnb52

**The best part of Les Baux is the château at the top,** where you can see the remains of the old fortifications, the dungeon, and all that good castle stuff. There are also working examples of some of the old-time weapons, like battering rams and catapults. These are demonstrated throughout the day and are very popular with kids.

I remember visiting the day after French President Nicolas Sarkozy lost his bid for reelection. The technician loaded a big water balloon into a catapult, said "Goodbye Nicolas!" and shot it off into space. I guess he wasn't a fan of Sarko.

**The views from the top are spectacular**, one of the best in Provence. You can see vineyards and olive groves, the Alpilles Mountains, and little villages and farmhouses here and there. Even if you are not a fan of castles or battering rams, just come and enjoy the view.

There is parking at the base of the town, as well as along the roads leading up to it. The earlier you get there, the closer you will be able to park. It is only a short walk from Les Baux to the Carrières de Lumières so you should **try to combine a visit to both.**

If you want to stay near Les Baux, one of the best hotels in Provence is Benvengudo*. It has beautiful grounds and an excellent restaurant, plus an inviting terrace if you'd like to stop by for a drink.

---

\*      tinyurl.com/y8l2wjdx

Les Baux's tourist office* is at the Maison du Roy on Rue Porte Mage†.

*Pro tip:* bring something to drink and maybe a snack when you visit the château above the village because there's not much available up there.

## Maussane-les-Alpilles for the Best Olive Oil

A few miles south of Les Baux, at the foot of the Alpilles, sits this small village surrounded by olive groves. Val and I love its central square, Place Joseph Laugier‡, filled with tables from the surrounding cafés and with a big fountain in the middle. The square is the perfect place to go for a relaxing meal or a drink, and you'll see people enjoying it at just about any hour of the day.

Maussane has a nice outdoor market on Thursday mornings, under shady plane trees, so try to go on that day if you can.

An interesting side trip is to explore the Castillon Towers§, three dilapidated medieval fortifications that used to protect Maussane and the southern flank of the Alpilles. They are about two miles south of town.

---

\*    tinyurl.com/47b6zdap

†    tinyurl.com/ycphvdfy

‡    tinyurl.com/48tknpxh

§    tinyurl.com/h5a9efpn

Maussane's tourist office[*] is on the Avenue des Alpilles[†] next to the Camping les Romarins.

## Shopping

For prepared Provençal food products, like tapenade and caviar d'aubergine, **one of the best shops in Provence** is the Jean Martin boutique[‡] at 9 rue Charloun Rieu[§]. It's a five-minute walk from the main square. You can get anything you need for an aperitif, plus there are soups, sauces, main dishes, you name it. You can also join a cooking class if you are feeling ambitious.

A few steps further down the street[¶], Moulin Cornille[**] has excellent **olive oil**. Or you can stop at Moulin Castelas[††], just outside of town[‡‡], for a fun and well-organized olive oil tasting[§§], plus a wide variety of great olive oils.

If you are looking to buy wine, there is a shop in town with an excellent selection, La caviste de Maussane at 60 Avenue de la Vallée des Baux[¶¶]. You can taste wines and

---

[*]   tinyurl.com/b29ucthn
[†]   tinyurl.com/4jdutzep
[‡]   tinyurl.com/vsnp96uj
[§]   tinyurl.com/472nckuj
[¶]   tinyurl.com/4h22evrk
[**]  tinyurl.com/hhefnzpz
[††]  tinyurl.com/ysbsjvv8
[‡‡]  tinyurl.com/9xmcp897
[§§]  tinyurl.com/2npbfasx
[¶¶]  tinyurl.com/4ez47yrc

get advice from the owner in just about any language you want—he speaks five (go ahead, try out your Swedish.)

## Where to Eat

A short walk off the square, at 87 Avenue de la Vallée des Baux[*], is one of my favorite restaurants in Provence, Le Clos Saint-Roch[†]. The food is delicious and the prices are reasonable—the chef is a *Maître Restauranteur* and has **won awards for "best value" restaurant**. He told me once, "Every day my cooking has to be great." I love the restaurant's outdoor courtyard on a warm day, and the inside is equally comfortable. This used to be a hangout of the late French singing legend Charles Aznavour, who lived nearby. I like the restaurant so much I dedicated an article to it[‡].

Right on the square[§] is another excellent restaurant run by a *Maître Restauranteur*, L'Oustaloun[¶]. You can eat on the square, or inside under the arched stone ceiling of what was once a 16th century abbey. The menu is compact and excellent, with an emphasis on traditional Provençal dishes. The restaurant is attached to a small hotel if you are looking for a place to stay.

---

[*]   tinyurl.com/a2eyhcc  

[†]   tinyurl.com/ytab4uff

[‡]   tinyurl.com/y8kx7qe8

[§]   tinyurl.com/y37r5rmz

[¶]   tinyurl.com/3jb8nhnf

For a quick, simple meal with tables on the square[*], we like Piazza del Gusto[†]. **Its menu is mostly pizza and pasta** and sometimes that hits the spot.

# Fontvieille

Fontvieille is a typically Provençal village with a shady central square, an old lavoir (clothes-washing basin), and a bustling open-air market on Monday mornings. Its tourist office[*] is on the Avenue des Moulins[§].

Fontvieille is a delightful place to spend a few hours and I especially like that it's the perfect base for exploring three nearby sites.

## Daudet's Windmill

The first is Daudet's windmill, about a half mile south of Fontvieille[¶] on the D33 (on the left.)

Alphonse Daudet is a beloved French author who spent much of his life in the South of France. His best-known work, *Letters from my Windmill,* tells tales of Provençal life—a mixture of day-to-day events and local folklore. The windmill still exists and is **a popular destination for lovers of French literature.**

---

[*] tinyurl.com/dsdwuyne
[†] tinyurl.com/5n6tsjnm
[*] tinyurl.com/3dywmkzy
[§] tinyurl.com/5ajv59u2
[¶] tinyurl.com/a897f7u

## The Greatest Power of the Ancient World

Next are the remains of a Roman aqueduct, part of an elaborate system that brought water to nearby Arles. It's about two miles south of Fontvieille[*] on the D82.

Water would travel through the aqueduct and then have to go down a steep, rocky hillside to continue its journey. "Why not take advantage of this?" thought the clever Romans.

Their engineers designed a series of mills[†] that the water raced through, one after another, as it tumbled down the hillside. The power they generated could mill grain for 12,000 people a day! Historians call it, "**the greatest concentration of mechanical power in the ancient world.**" You can see a mockup of it in the Museum of Ancient Arles[‡].

## Montmajour Abbey

From the end of the aqueduct, at the top of the hill, you can look far across the fields[§] and see Montmajour Abbey[¶]. It was a favorite of Vincent van Gogh and he painted it several times.

The abbey is no longer in use but is well worth a visit. It sits on top of a huge rock, which seems awkward until

---

[*] tinyurl.com/rucdavue
[†] tinyurl.com/hbwfju7e
[‡] tinyurl.com/rpx2uwcn
[§] tinyurl.com/4pcp3t4j
[¶] tinyurl.com/yjr46tar

you realize that at the time it was built, it was the only spot above water. The surrounding countryside was all marshland that has since been drained and turned over to agriculture. I like to stand on that big rock and look around, imagining what the world was like back in olden times, when the abbey was sitting alone in the middle of the marsh.

# Arles

Arles was a major city in the Roman Empire so it is included in the section Roman Provence.

# The Alpilles Mountains and their Châteaux

*Les Alpilles* ("the little Alps") are a small mountain range south of St-Rémy, running east to west for about 15 miles. Their north flank rises up sharply from a flat landscape, making the Alpilles look bigger than they really are and providing a dramatical backdrop to St-Rémy. The book *The Alpilles from the Air* offers a birds-eye view of the Alpilles in all their glory*.

The Alpilles form the heart of a nature preserve, the Alpilles Natural Regional Park, and are crisscrossed with **wonderful hiking trails**. The small roads that run through them are quiet, and a **good place for bike rides**. See the Activities section below for some of my favorite hikes and bike routes.

The Alpilles are near the confluence of two major rivers, the Rhône and the Durance, plus they lie at the intersection of several roads dating back to the days of the Romans. Because of their strategic location, they are dotted with numerous châteaux (fortresses) that were built to levy tolls on traders using the rivers and roads. The history of these châteaux is very interesting, and many can be visited[†].

---

*     tinyurl.com/yc6jmnyc
†     tinyurl.com/y22ykrmv

# East of St-Rémy

## The Romanin Glider Airport

Four miles east of St-Rémy[*] is a small airport called the Aérodrome de Romanin[†] where gliders take off and land. If you look up, you can often see them soaring over the Alpilles.

Val and I like to ride our bikes to the aerodrome and **watch the gliders take off.** They are launched by a contraption that's like a gigantic fishing reel, with a long cable wrapped around it. This gets unwound and a cable more than half a mile long is attached to the glider.

When the ready signal is given—zip!—the contraption starts spinning, rewinding the cable and pulling the glider at high speed. Within seconds, the plane is airborne, climbing higher and higher until the cable is released. It has a little parachute on it so it comes down safely.

---

[*]    tinyurl.com/5b5v8p8m  🌐
[†]    tinyurl.com/wx6864k

The aerodrome is a big grassy field and sometimes the grass gets too long for safe takeoffs and landings. So, a few times a year it is closed and a local shepherd comes by with his flock to "mow" it.

We met the shepherd once, while the sheep were doing their mowing, and he told us about his sheepdogs. "These little ones here are very smart and know how to keep the sheep in line, while those big guys over there are real lunkheads. But I need them in the summer when we head to the mountains—they protect the flock from wolves." I guess everyone has their specialty!

**If you are interested in going on a glider ride** (with an experienced pilot, of course), you can arrange it via the Aéroclub de St Rémy des Alpilles*. They are open every day of the year, weather permitting. To book your flight, send an e-mail to contact@aeroclub-alpilles.fr with the following information:

- First name, last name
- Desired date of flight (or week)
- Morning or afternoon
- Number of people flying

Or call +33 (0)4 90 92 08 43 from 8:00 to noon, and 1:30pm to 4:30pm Monday to Friday.

---

\*   tinyurl.com/52me9cp3

# Eygalières and a Hero of the French Resistance

About eight miles east of St-Rémy is the village of Eygalières. It's small—practically a hamlet—and is an unusual combination of rustic and chic.

There's only one main street, a few hundred yards long, and it has everything a Provençal village should have. There's a butcher, a boulangerie, a newsstand, some bars and cafés—all the usual stuff. Sometimes you'll see a horse hitched to a post while its owner stops for coffee. Eygalières has an excellent market on Friday mornings with everything you need.

The other thing the main street has is a surprising number of real estate agents. Eygalières has become a favorite of France's rich and famous, some of whom have second homes in the area. You might spot one from time to time, though they are more likely to be in one of the fancy restaurants or hotels outside the main part of town.

**The most popular tourist spot** in Eygalières is the Sainte Sixte chapel*, one of the most-photographed sites in the area. It sits on a rocky knoll about a mile outside of town, with excellent views all around.

Eygalières is famous in French history as the place where Resistance hero Jean Moulin† hid after parachuting into the Alpilles on a freezing winter night. He had been tasked

---

\*     tinyurl.com/35v2mdkf 🌐

†     tinyurl.com/43utncmb

by Charles de Gaulle to combine the different French Resistance groups into one, which he successfully did before he was murdered by the Nazis. The farmhouse where he hid is just outside of town, with a small plaque commemorating Moulin. The next day he walked from there to the town of Saint-Andiol, and a building there has a huge portrait of him painted on the side, visible from the D7 road. The route he took is commemorated today, as the road between Eygalières and the D99 is marked as both *Route Jean Moulin* and *Chemin de la Liberté*.

The Eygalières tourist office does not have a physical presence but does have a website[*].

## Where to Eat

There are plenty of restaurants in town, ranging from hearty and basic to fancy and expensive, but my favorite is a friendly little place on the main street[†] called Restaurant Paulette[‡].

The fabulous website Perfectly Provence has a helpful list of recommended restaurants in Eygalières[§].

---

[*]   tinyurl.com/mwzpx852

[†]   tinyurl.com/k6rd8k9a

[‡]   tinyurl.com/9bbtkxan

[§]   tinyurl.com/yeh5c8fx

# The Giant Melon Statue

A dozen miles east of St-Rémy is the town of Cavaillon. You might visit it to see the old synagogue (see the Jewish Provence section). Or maybe you are daring and want to dangle from a mountainside on the Via Ferrata[*]. Or perhaps you are going to catch a movie at one of the town's two theaters, the Cinéma La Cigale and the Cinéma Femina.

In any case, as you arrive from St-Rémy, you'll come to a large traffic circle. As you go around it, you'll see a big round thing off to your right[†] and wonder, "What the heck is that?"

The answer: it's a big melon. More precisely, a giant melon statue that **weighs nine tons**. But this isn't any

---

[*]   tinyurl.com/vbwby6xt
[†]   tinyurl.com/hjw7kr68

old melon, oh no. This is a *melon de Cavaillon*, the best melon in France.

If you are in France during melon season, you have to try one because it will be **the best melon you've ever had**. Alexandre Dumas, the author of *The Three Musketeers*, was such a fan that he once sent the Cavaillon library a complete set of his books in exchange for a "pension" of 12 melons a year…for life!

Cavaillon treats its melons with reverence. The town's top restaurant, Prévôt*, offers a "melon menu" where every dish includes the famous fruit. The melon has its own festival, the *Féria du Melon*, which culminates in the running of 100 white Camargue horses through town. And the official Brotherhood of the Knights of the Cavaillon Melon (*Confrérie des Chevaliers de l'Ordre du Melon de Cavaillon*) ensures top quality through a rigorous process of testing and evaluation.

You know a town is crazy about something when they erect a statue in its honor, and that's exactly what Cavaillon has done.

---

\*     tinyurl.com/3mcr3pmt

# West of St-Rémy

## The Calenquet Olive Mill

Olive oil has been produced in St-Rémy since ancient times—the first Christian king of France, Clovis, was baptized using St-Rémy olive oil in the year 496.

If you'd like to see an operating mill and do some **olive oil tasting**, be sure to visit the Moulin du Calenquet*, a few miles west of town on the Vieux Chemin d'Arles†. If you've never done an olive oil tasting, it's interesting to find how different the various oils taste, and how some give you a little burn on the back of your throat. The mill's shop also sells olives (of course) and various olive-based products like tapenade.

If you would prefer just to taste and buy, there's also a shop in St-Rémy, at 8 rue de la Commune‡.

---

\*    tinyurl.com/eyb4xmuw
†    tinyurl.com/5upvyt32
‡    tinyurl.com/hk75z82y

# The Monster of Tarascon

If you go west from St-Rémy for about ten miles, you'll come to the town of Tarascon on the banks of the Rhône River. It has an impressive fortress that used to collect tolls from boats going up and down the Rhône. One sneaky ruler once pledged the fortress as collateral for several different loans from several different people, hoping that none of them found out about the others.

The town is named after a legendary monster called the Tarasque, a huge beast which lived in the river and occasionally came out to eat people. There are various descriptions of it, but my favorite says it breathed fire and belched so much smoke that its head was surrounded by a blue cloud with red lightning bolts.

The Tarasque was finally subdued by Saint Martha, and Saint Martha's Collegiate Church[*] is said to guard her earthly remains. About a hundred yards from it[†] is a statue of the Tarasque, which I find disappointingly non-fearsome—I think it looks like a giant armadillo with a bad haircut[‡].

Every year the town holds a big festival on the last weekend in June that includes a procession with a mockup of the Tarasque, so be sure to go if you are in the area.

For other interesting local legends, like the one about Mary Magdalene in Provence (remember *The Da Vinci Code*?) be sure to read the section of this book called Legends of Provence.

There is no official tourist website for Tarascon but there is a pretty good unofficial one[§].

---

[*]    tinyurl.com/t3aydy9n
[†]    tinyurl.com/x8mu6fxz
[‡]    tinyurl.com/atakytxr
[§]    tinyurl.com/6fr6az3y

# Activities

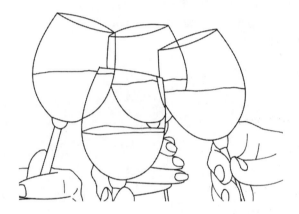

## My Favorite Wineries

Provence is a wine lover's paradise, and wines have been produced here for thousands of years. There are excellent wineries in and around St-Rémy, and here are some of my favorites. They all have English-speaking staff.

## Château Romanin

Wine has been produced here for millennia, going back to the days of the Greeks. And it is a place steeped in mysticism, where druids worshipped their ancient gods*.

In the 13th century, a Templar knight built his great château here, on a rocky outcropping of the Alpilles. It was not only his fortress but also a Court of Love, where noble ladies presided over "questions of gallantry." I wonder, could you be thrown in the dungeon for not picking up a lady's hanky? Or get fifty lashes for using the wrong fork?

The château is now a ruin but nearby is the most beautiful winery in the area, Château Romanin. **Be sure to tour the underground "cathedral winery"** (reservations required.) The tasting room is beautiful and the wines are outstanding, maybe the best in the area, with prices to match.

---

* tinyurl.com/y8ghfj7l

## Château Romanin[*]

Route de Cavaillon (D99)[†]
Saint-Rémy-de-Provence
Contact: +33 (0)4 90 92 69 57 or
accueil@ChateauRomanin.fr

Tours can also be organized through Wine Tour Booking[‡].

# Domaine des Terres Blanches

A bit further east, this is another top winery with a friendly tasting room. **I especially like their white wine made with a healthy dose of the Rolle grape** (elsewhere called Vermentino.) Besides the wines, there are also local products sold in the tasting room.

## Domaine des Terres Blanches[§]

Route de Cavaillon (D99)[¶]
Saint-Rémy-de-Provence
Contact: +33 (0)4 90 95 91 66 or
info@terresblanches.com

---

[*]   tinyurl.com/55vk73nr
[†]   tinyurl.com/ppvw3vky
[‡]   tinyurl.com/p4r465c
[§]   tinyurl.com/sd34d9m
[¶]   tinyurl.com/juppftj6

## Mas de la Dame

The medieval seer Nostradamus, who was born in St-Rémy, once prophesied that "one day the sea will cover the earth, and will stop at the stele of Mas de la Dame." You can still see the stele, and water is not yet lapping at its foot, but maybe you should visit the winery soon in case Nostradamus was right.

Mas de la Dame is south of St-Rémy, off the D5, about a half mile after you've gone over the Alpilles on the way to Maussane.

**The view from the road leading into the winery is spectacular**. I like to stop there sometimes and gaze up at those beautiful mountains.

The large tasting room serves a wide variety of wines, and you can also buy olive oil and other local products.

**Mas de la Dame**[*]

Chemin Départemental 5 (D5)[†]
Les Baux de Provence
Contact: +33 (0)4 90 54 32 24 or
masdeladame@masdeladame.com

---

[*]    tinyurl.com/377s7ttb
[†]    tinyurl.com/4h689j6w

## Mas Sainte Berthe

Nestled below the towering château of Les Baux, this is my go-to winery for rosé wines. All the wines are good here, but **I especially like the rosés.**

The tasting room is small and friendly, with a boutique attached where you can buy olive oil and other local products. The winery is about two miles from Mas de la Dame, off of the D27A heading to Les Baux.

Some of Sainte Berthe's wines can be purchased not only in bottles, but also in a five or ten liter "bag-in-box." BIB wines have a reputation for low quality, but there are plenty of good ones in France. I sometimes keep a BIB in the fridge, to have a glass of wine in the afternoon—they last about three weeks after opening.

**Mas Sainte Berthe**[*]

Chemin de Sainte Berthe[†]
Les Baux de Provence
Contact: +33 (0)4 90 54 39 01 or
mas@sainteberthe.com

---

[*]    tinyurl.com/3jsyyxrk
[†]    tinyurl.com/v8cef8c2

## Drink Like a Roman

One of the most interesting wineries* in Provence is the Mas des Tourelles, near Beaucaire. Once a Roman villa, then a winery of great renown, part of it has now been made into an authentic Roman vineyard and winery. You can take a tour, see a video on Roman winemaking techniques, then taste wines made using ancient Roman recipes. Some are sweet and pleasant, with honey used as an ingredient. Others are, shall we say, "interesting." Fenugreek in your wine, anyone?

Mas des Tourelles makes for an interesting stop for lovers of history and of wine alike. There is grape juice for the kids and a room full of Roman games that everyone can play.

**Mas des Tourelles**†

4294 Route de Saint-Gilles‡
Beaucaire
Contact: +33 (0)4 66 59 19 72

---

\*      tinyurl.com/2mz2vzdj
†      tinyurl.com/ywzcfek4
‡      tinyurl.com/ytsrczfe

# Special Picnic Spots

Val and I like to bring our lunch when we hike or bike, stopping *n'importe où* (anywhere) for a picnic. There are plenty of beautiful spots for picnicking near St-Rémy, and here are two of our favorites.

## Lac du Peiroou

Ten minutes from the center of St-Rémy[*] is a shady picnic spot popular with the locals[†]. It sits along the shore of a lake created thousands of years ago by the Romans.

Lac du Peiroou is a small reservoir, created by a dam that spans a narrow gap between two rocky outcroppings. While the current dam was built a century ago, the original dates back to the first century B.C., when the Romans built it to supply water to Glanum.

---

[*]    tinyurl.com/apbdtwj9  🌐
[†]    tinyurl.com/yajavf73

The lake has a wide, grassy area at one end, with trees that provide **welcome shade on a sunny Provençal day**. It's the perfect place to spread out a blanket and enjoy a lazy afternoon.

### Near Aureille

About a mile north of Aureille, on the D25A, is a small dirt parking lot on the side of the road called Parkplatz Klettern* (who knows why the name is in German.) There is a beautiful view of the mountains and you can often see rock climbers on the nearby slopes.

Next to the parking lot are olive trees surrounded by rough grass—be sure to bring something to sit on. It's a great spot for a picnic.

# My Favorite Hiking Trails

Here are three of my favorite ways to get some exercise, from easiest to hardest (though none is very hard.)

### Canal Walks

For a shady, pretty walk, there's nothing like strolling along the paths that line the region's many canals. See the A Cool Walk on a Hot Day section for more details.

---

\*    tinyurl.com/ysjuxmuu    🌐

# From the Romanin Glider Airport to the Roman Bridge

This is a pretty walk that goes along the base of the Alpilles and is flat and mostly shady. You pass some vineyards and get nice views of the mountains. It's about three miles round trip and very pleasant. However, **it's not very well marked.**

To start, park at the Romanin Aerodrome[*] and walk towards the side of the aerodrome closest to the mountains. You'll see a shed with a metal roof and open sides, sitting on a little rise. Walk towards it, then to the left until you see a little path towards the mountains. Follow it and you'll shortly come to a trail that you take to the left.

Follow this for about a mile and a half. You'll come to a little old stone bridge that the locals call the Roman bridge[†]. It's a nice little bridge, very sturdy, but I'm sorry to tell you that it's not Roman. It crosses what is usually a dry ditch that only fills with water after heavy rains. Next to it is a dirt parking lot and beyond that the D24 road. This is where you turn around.

An alternative is to start at the Roman bridge and take the route in reverse. The dirt parking lot is marked by a sign with a picture of a hiker, on the edge of the D24 road.

For me, the best part of the walk is going through the vineyards near the aerodrome because there are **great views of the mountains as well as of the vineyards**.

---

[*]   tinyurl.com/5b5v8p8m  

[†]   tinyurl.com/4556fwhj  

One of my all-time favorite photos is of Val here with our dog Mica, both of them looking gloriously happy in the warm sunshine.

## Up to La Caume

My favorite hike is the one to up La Caume, one of the highest points in the Alpilles, and **the views are excellent**. I guess you could start at the bottom of the Alpilles and climb all the way up but I'm not that sporty. I like to start partway up the mountain and hike on the asphalt-covered trails. The main thing to watch out for is the heat because there is not a lot of shade. If it's a warm day I start early and **always take plenty of water.**

My starting point is the Parking de la Caume[*], a lot at the crest of the D5, the road that goes up and over the Alpilles from St-Rémy to Maussane. The parking lot is on the left when heading out of St. Remy, and is easy to miss, so go slowly as you get toward the top.

From the parking lot, head out the back (the side opposite from the D5) and start walking. The trail is gravel at first but quickly becomes paved. Along the side are occasional signs identifying the plants you are passing.

There are some gravel roads leading off to one side or the other, but ignore them and stay on the paved trail. There are a few somewhat steep sections but they are not too bad, except the very last part that will have you huffing a bit. It starts just after you pass a rusty sign

---

[*]    tinyurl.com/4pz43xd2   🌐

marked La Caume, so if you want to avoid it, you can turn around here.

It's a little more than two miles to the top and takes about 45 minutes each way. Along the route you'll get excellent views to the north, over St-Rémy and the surrounding countryside. There's an **especially good view of the *Rocher des deux trous***, the famous giant rock with two big holes in it that is visible from St-Rémy. You can see it if you go about 30 yards past the La Caume sign, turn around, and look slightly to your right. You can also walk out to the *Rocher*, taking a path that starts near the La Caume sign—the views from it are fabulous.

The very top of the trail, at La Caume, is somewhat marred by a giant communications tower, but the views are fabulous. On a clear day you can see nearly to the Mediterranean Sea.

## My Favorite Bike Routes

Val and I love to bike in and around the Alpilles, on routes that range from easy to moderately difficult.

If you stay off the busy main roads, biking in the Alpilles is easy and safe. There are a number of shops that rent bikes, in St-Rémy and nearby. Sun E-bike*, with multiple locations, is known for **electric bike rentals**. Alpilles13† has **electric bike rental shops** in both St-Rémy‡ and Eygalières§.

With the increasing popularity of electric bikes, there are more and more bike paths being built, like the one from St-Rémy to Mollegès Gare that runs just north of the D99 road. Check with your local tourist office for the latest information.

Here are some of our favorite routes, from easiest to hardest. There are more challenging circuits as well, with markings along the route, and there is lots of mountain biking you can do in the Alpilles—check at your local tourist office for more information. There is also information on biking in the Resources section of this book.

---

*  tinyurl.com/5bn4z28k
†  tinyurl.com/22n8bkf7
‡  tinyurl.com/2bhhmx6x
§  tinyurl.com/ytccabhv

# From St-Rémy to the Romanin Glider Airport

This route is about seven miles round trip. It's a nice, flat ride and the best part is watching the gliders take off and land at the aerodrome.

You can see the route on Google Maps[*].

Start by going east from the arena[†] on Avenue Folco de Baroncelli. This road changes names a few times and eventually becomes Ancien Voie Aurelia, which takes you to the edge of the aerodrome.

The tricky part about this route is that it makes a jog at about the halfway point and **you can easily miss it.** Here's how not to: After you've gone about a mile and a half and you see a vineyard on your left, be alert. At the far end of the vineyard, turn right at Cours des Guillots and then take an immediate left to stay on the Ancien Voie Aurelia.

Follow this to an intersection where you can see that it becomes a dirt road just beyond the intersection. Don't continue onto the dirt part but instead take the road to the right, which takes you into the aerodrome.

If you look up, you'll see one of the best wineries in the area, Château Romanin[‡], in the hills above the aerodrome.

---

[*]  tinyurl.com/y9a9bt3n
[†]  tinyurl.com/rzxsd4c
[‡]  tinyurl.com/y8ghfj7l

## From St-Rémy to Saint-Étienne-du-Grès

This route is about 12 miles round trip. Saint-Étienne is west of St-Rémy and the road is mostly flat. It's a nice ride, past orchards and vineyards, and in the springtime you'll see fields of poppies. The very last stretch is a moderately steep descent so **if you don't want to climb up on the return**, turn around when you get to the downhill.

You can see the route on Google Maps[*].

The majority of the route is along the Vieux Chemin d'Arles (Old Arles Road). To get there, go to the parking lot across from the church in St-Rémy. From there, take the Chemin de la Combette until it intersects[†] the Vieux Chemin d'Arles, then turn right.

## From Eygalières to Aureille

This route is about 13 miles round trip and has wonderful views of the Alpilles, plus a chance to see **rock climbers doing their thing**.

You can see the route on Google Maps[‡].

From Eygalières, take the D248 west until it dead ends at the D24. Turn left. You'll start a gradual ascent with a great view of the Alpilles. Follow this for about a mile, where you'll come to the intersection of the D24 and

---

[*]    tinyurl.com/4kuxx53n
[†]    tinyurl.com/ykwrc7wu
[‡]    tinyurl.com/hetc3p4w

the D25. Stay left to get on the D25 (stay on the same road; it just changes numbers.)

Follow this for another mile until the D25A goes off to the right with signs pointing to Aureille. This begins a steep section but it's only about a quarter-mile long before it flattens out and then descends. Continue for another mile or so beyond that, through a narrow section with a rock wall on one side, then emerge from that and enjoy great views of the mountains.

On your left, look for a little dirt parking lot, the Parkplatz Klettern* that usually has a few cars in it. If you stand in the lot with your back to the road and look up into the mountains to your left, you can often see climbers on the rocks. Very cool! (you'll never find me up there, I'm scared of heights) Val and I sometimes like to picnic here, in the grassy areas around the olive trees, and enjoy the view.

If you continue another mile, you'll get to Aureille, a cute little town with the ruins of a medieval château looming over the place. There are a few places here to get something to eat or drink.

## From Eygalières to Eyguières

This route is about 20 miles long and begins the same way as the Eygalières to Aureille route. But instead of turning off the D25 onto the D25A to go to Aureille, you continue straight on the D25.

---

*    tinyurl.com/ysjuxmuu

You can see the route on Google Maps[*].

There are great mountain views here and sometimes I feel like I'm right in the middle of the Alpilles; I love this ride. **One caution** on the route: there's a big, looping curve about a half mile past the Aureille turnoff. The views are great but it's a blind curve and cars sometimes take it too fast, so proceed with caution on this stretch.

After this big curve, you'll climb for a while and then descend, followed by a flat stretch leading to Eyguières. I find the flat stretch boring so I usually turn around when the descent begins.

## To Hell and Back
## (the route to the Val d'Enfer)

If you are feeling energetic, you can do some climbing and get one of the best views in Provence at the Val d'Enfer (Hell Valley.) This route is about 10 miles round trip, or 16 miles round trip if you go all the way to Maussane-les-Alpilles.

You can see the shorter route on Google Maps[†].

You can see the longer route on Google Maps[‡].

To get to the Val d'Enfer, begin on the route from St-Rémy to Saint-Étienne-du-Grès. (see above.) When you are a bit over a mile from St-Rémy, you'll come to a stop

---

[*]   tinyurl.com/5bzd75ac  

[†]   tinyurl.com/ynjh3fuz  ⊕

[‡]   tinyurl.com/trvvh2n3  ⊕

sign at the Route des Baux (D27.) Turn left here and you'll soon start climbing. The ascent gets steeper as you go, with some switchbacks near the top, and if you are like me you might stop a few times to catch your breath.

After about three miles, you hit the top (hurray!) with some very nice views off to the right. Enjoy them, then keep going a little further for the *great* view.** The road will descend steeply and make a sharp right turn. Park your bike at this turn and cross the road for a **fabulous view of Les Baux-de-Provence**. There might be other people there because it's a popular view spot. If you want to drive, there's a small parking lot across the road,

You can continue a bit further along the road to see the craggy rock formations that give Hell Valley its name, but be aware that you'll soon come to the very popular Carrières de Lumières† immersive art show. This draws a lot of traffic so you might want to turn around before you get here. If you want to continue, go on to Maussane-les-Alpilles, which is about three miles away.

To do this, pass the Carrières de Lumières and stay right at the fork a few hundred yards later. This is the D27 and you'll begin a descent that's about a mile long. Enjoy the views on both sides—up to Les Baux on your left and down to the rocky valley on your right.

At the bottom of the hill, turn left to stay on the D27 and follow it for about a mile and a half to Maussane.

---

\*    tinyurl.com/3z28w6p9   🌐

†    tinyurl.com/y62xzqcg

You've now gone up and over the Alpilles and will need to do it again on your return. Time for sustenance! The good news is that Maussane is full of great cafés and restaurants, many of them near the town's central square. Check out the Maussane-les-Alpilles section of this book to see my favorites.

**As an alternative to continuing straight, if you still have the energy, turn left and go up a steep road that goes about a quarter of a mile and then ends. From there, you'll see a stretch of rock that you walk up for about 50 yards, at the top of which is **possibly the most magnificent view in Provence**—on a clear day you can see Mont Ventoux, Mont Sainte-Victoire, the Mediterranean Sea and everything in between. This spot* supposedly has an orientation table but it's not really there anymore.

## From Maussane-les-Alpilles to Eygalières

This route is about 22 miles round trip, with some hills, but you can go only as far as you want and then turn around. I like it because it's got everything†—olive groves, vineyards, forests, the Alpilles. It goes past Mas de Gourgonnier‡ § if you want to do some wine tasting along the way.

You can see the route on Google Maps⁋.

---

This route passes the famous spot where Resistance hero Jean Moulin parachute-landed in the middle of a cold winter's night. Sometimes you see **giant letters JM** carved into the foliage on a hillside, commemorating the event.

Start at the intersection of the D5 and the D17 in Maussane* and head east towards Mouriès. Get off this road after about 200 yards because it's very busy, and take the D5 to the left. The first thing you pass is a big barn with farmyard animals—you might smell them before you see them. After about a half a mile, there's a road that goes off to the right. Ignore it and continue straight, where the D5 changes to the D78.

Take this for about four miles, through olive groves and vineyards, with one short but very steep section where I sometimes walk my bike. The D78 then dead-ends at the D24. Turn left here and you will soon be in a forest. I once saw a shepherd and his sheep along the side of the road, along with a couple of sheepdogs that kept an eye on me.

This part climbs for about two miles and then starts a descent. After about a mile there is an intersection where you go left to stay on the D24. Follow this for another mile or so and enjoy the nice downhill glide, then follow the signs and turn right to go to Eygalières. There are plenty of cafés in town if you'd like to stop for lunch before you begin your return trip—see the section of this book on Eygalières for more details.

---

\*    tinyurl.com/f7a4rbwn

# Avignon and its Popes

## The History of the Popes

For centuries, popes jockeyed with kings and emperors for worldly power. This competition came to a head in the early 14th century, when Pope Boniface VIII excommunicated French King Philip IV (note to Boniface: bad idea.) Before long, forces loyal to the king attacked and beat the pope, who died soon after.

Boniface's successor was short-lived, and King Philip forced the next papal conclave to elect a friend of his as Pope Clement V. Clement refused to go to Rome. Instead, he set up shop in Avignon—the city and surrounding territories then making up the French Papal States. Thus began the Avignon Papacy, or as some in Rome snidely call it today, the Babylonian Captivity.

From 1309 to 1376, a series of seven popes held court in Avignon and—surprise!—all of them were French. It was these popes who built the enormous Papal Palace, as well as the massive walls around the city.

Further north, they built a summer palace near a town that became known as Châteauneuf-du-Pape ("the pope's new château.") They covered the surrounding countryside with vineyards because, well, popes need to drink. Today Châteauneuf-du-Pape produces some of France's greatest wines.

Things began to fall apart in 1376 when Pope Gregory IX decided to move back to Rome. After he died, competing groups of cardinals elected two different popes, one in Rome and one in Avignon. This "Western Schism," with its competing popes, continued until 1417 when Church leadership was finally unified. The popes elected in Avignon after 1376 are now considered antipopes and, not surprisingly, no troublemaking Frenchman has been elected to the papacy since.

## The Papal Palace

Both a fortress and a palace, the Papal Palace[*][†] is one of the largest and **most important medieval Gothic buildings in Europe**. It is actually two buildings joined together—an older fortress/palace built on the impregnable Rock of Doms, and a newer and more lavish palace built by one of the Avignon popes.

---

[*]  tinyurl.com/4rcc6s7r

[†]  tinyurl.com/c6pyb6w

## The Ramparts

These massive walls are one of the **finest examples of medieval fortifications** anywhere. They can be seen throughout the city but the most dramatic are along the side facing the Rhône River. When I look at them, I realize how insecure life was in the Middle Ages, when even popes needed gigantic walls to keep them safe.

## The Pont d'Avignon

You might remember the children's song about this famous bridge ("*Sur le Pont d'Avignon, l'on y danse, l'on y danse.*") Formally known as the Pont Saint-Bénézet[*] it was completed shortly before the Avignon Papacy. It connected the city to the town of Villeneuve-lès-Avignon on the other side of the Rhône, where the cardinals built their palaces.

Sadly, only a small part of the original structure remains, and visitors are often disappointed by this little stub of a bridge. But fear not! A team of French historians recently **recreated the original bridge** in 3D, in a fascinating video[†].

---

[*]   tinyurl.com/wzu7c3f9

[†]   tinyurl.com/bbcvpxc

# The Best View of Avignon

There is a big island in the middle of the Rhône River, the Île de la Barthelasse[*] and the views from there to Avignon are fabulous. **A great place for a picnic** is the long, grassy esplanade facing the Pont d'Avignon. Or you can enjoy a meal at Restaurant le Bercail[†][‡] with tables right along the water. There is a lot to do on the island, and you can reach it by foot, ferry, or car[§].

# Where to Eat

There are lots of cafés and restaurants in the bustling Place de l'Horloge[¶] the large square close to the Papal Palace. Want to try something different? Then go to the couscous restaurant Couscousserie de l'Horloge at 18 Place de l'Horloge[**]. And don't miss the chance to visit Les Halles[††] the local covered market. Choc-a-block with regional products – from luscious olives to *herbes de Provence*, cheeses, charcuterie and bread—Les Halles is the perfect place to stock up on gourmet goodies.

The Avignon tourist office[‡‡] is at 41 Cours Jean Jaurès[§§].

---

| | |
|---|---|
| * | tinyurl.com/3rpnestt 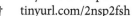 |
| † | tinyurl.com/2nsp2fsh |
| ‡ | tinyurl.com/339j4u52 |
| § | tinyurl.com/pezu9vsf |
| ¶ | tinyurl.com/axbxuk8j |
| ** | tinyurl.com/3sptcwjt |
| †† | tinyurl.com/57ewarhh |
| ‡‡ | tinyurl.com/ns7hevcm |
| §§ | tinyurl.com/2xpnbxdk  |

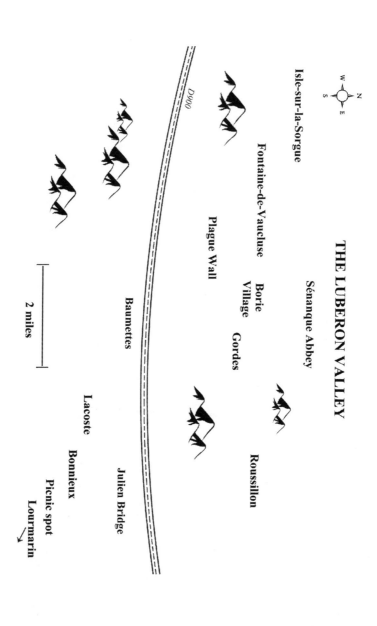

THE LUBERON VALLEY

Isle-sur-la-Sorgue

N
W — E
S

D900

Sénanque Abbey

Fontaine-de-Vaucluse

Borie
Village

Gordes

Plague Wall

Roussillon

Baumettes

2 miles

Lacoste

Bonnieux

Julien Bridge

Picnic spot

Lourmarin

# The Luberon Valley

The Luberon Valley is the setting of Peter Mayle's delightful book, *A Year in Provence*. It's a beautiful region and has everything Provence is known for, from charming hilltop villages to sun-dappled lavender fields to old men playing pétanque.

This section of the book will proceed around the region in a roughly clockwise direction, starting with l'Isle-sur-la-Sorgue.

# Highlights

- The abandoned ochre quarries of Roussillon are **a riot of color:** red, purple, orange, and yellow. Walk through them and marvel at the colorful cliffs.

- Fontaine de Vaucluse is one of the world's largest springs, bursting forth and forming the Sorgue River. It's like **the river comes out of nowhere!**

- **For quiet contemplation,** there's nothing like the austere Sénanque abbey, nestled in a little valley with a lavender field in front of it

- High above the hilltop village of Bonnieux is a **secret picnic spot** with views that go on forever

- On the road to Gordes is one of the **best photo spots** in Provence

- Coustellet and Velleron offer special "producer's" markets, where **the farmers themselves** offer their fresh produce

- The Café de France in Lacoste has good food and a **fabulous view**

- You can ride along a **flat, paved bike route** and see both a Neolithic burial chamber and an old Roman bridge, where you can enjoy a picnic

# l'Isle-sur-la-Sorgue, the Venice of France

Known as the Venice of France, the name of this town means "island in the Sorgue (river)." That's because the Sorgue runs around and through it, creating an island in the middle of town. Cafés and restaurants line the pretty river, and they are pleasant spots to have a meal or drink.

l'Isle-sur-la-Sorgue is the antiques center of Provence, so anyone looking for antiques can shop to their heart's content. In addition to the regular offerings, there are two gigantic antique fairs a year, at Easter and mid-August, where over 500 vendors offer their wares.

l'Isle-sur-la-Sorgue also has one of France's largest weekly markets, on Sunday morning, and be sure to **get there early** if you want to find parking. I park in the lot[*] next to the train station, because it's the biggest lot in town and there are usually open spaces. To find it, get on Avenue Julien Guigue and, at the circle in front of the station, go off to the right (as you face the station.)

When Val and I go to the market, we like to have coffee and people watch at the Café de France[†][‡] in the town's shady central square. It's also a good place for lunch. There are lots of restaurants along the banks of the Sorgue River, and my favorite is La Balade des Saveurs[§][¶].

---

[*]     tinyurl.com/4zsfaawh

[†]     tinyurl.com/4expjmms

[‡]     tinyurl.com/pkmk5vjj

[§]     tinyurl.com/yxncp2r9

[¶]     tinyurl.com/mrxzepvc

For excellent food I also love Restaurant La Libellule[*][†] and RENAUD'mets[‡][§]. For a memorable meal, consider Michelin-starred Le Vivier[ʃ][**] on the outskirts of town. It has outdoor tables and one of them is on a little bridge over the river—try to reserve that table if you can.

The town's tourist office[††] is at 13 Place Ferdinand Buisson[‡‡].

## Fontaine-de-Vaucluse and the River from Nowhere

This is one of my favorite spots in Provence[§§], where a river seems to appear out of nowhere.

The first time Val and I visited Fontaine-de-Vaucluse, we strolled through the pretty town that runs alongside the Sorgue River, then took the shady path upstream. We admired the Sorgue's brilliantly clear waters and gazed up at the remains of a medieval castle.

After a few hundred yards, I could see that we were headed towards the face of a cliff. "I wonder what the river does," I thought. "I guess it goes around the cliff."

Then we got to the cliff and there was no more river, just a pool of water, very blue-looking. It seemed still

---

[*] tinyurl.com/4x5r666f
[†] tinyurl.com/3shn825j
[‡] tinyurl.com/5hhfw32r
[§] tinyurl.com/4prk23fr
[ʃ] tinyurl.com/3z6pf4yp
[**] tinyurl.com/2p3uz2hp
[††] tinyurl.com/3f8back4
[‡‡] tinyurl.com/3a7adfb7
[§§] tinyurl.com/3vhw623c

and calm, but then we saw water was pouring out of one side, I mean *gushing*. It was creating the river, an entire river! That's a lot of water.

I found out later that this is **one of the largest springs in the world**, and that calm-looking pool is incredibly deep, almost 1,000 feet. The famous undersea explorer Jacques Cousteau once tried to dive down and find the bottom, but it was too deep even for him—he almost died in the attempt (a robot finally did the job.)

The best time to go is in the spring or after a rain, when the waters are at their peak, but the area and the town are pretty any time of year. There are plenty of nice restaurants along the water, plus an underground museum where you can see stalagmites and grottos, and the best santon museum in Provence.

For excellent food, my favorite restaurant is La Figuière[*][†]. For something more casual, I love Restaurant Philip[‡], a restaurant that sits alongside the river near the *fontaine* itself[§].

If you'd like to try a water sport (great on a hot day!) there are several kayak companies on the way into town. They have trips where you float down to l'Isle-sur-la-Sorgue and are easy enough for beginners.

The town's tourist office[¶] is on Avenue Robert Garcin[**].

---

[*]   tinyurl.com/jy99kr6f
[†]   tinyurl.com/kpxx9ute
[‡]   tinyurl.com/4dwc735j
[§]   tinyurl.com/mryfa8zz
[¶]   tinyurl.com/5xwf4fnu
[**]  tinyurl.com/v8hx6bfy

# The Plague Wall of Provence

300 years ago, the last great outbreak of bubonic plague hit France. It started in Marseille and spread north, toward the French Papal States and the Kingdom of France (Provence was then a separate territory.) So, the pope and the king decided to build a wall to stop it. Parts of this Plague Wall (*Mur de la Peste*)* are still there, near Cabrières d'Avignon.

The story of the plague is a depressingly familiar tale of human greed and folly. In 1720, a ship from the Middle East arrived in Marseille. Its cargo was destined for the annual trade fair in Beaucaire, then one of the largest in Europe. Plague had been detected on the ship, which normally would require a quarantine, but that would mean missing the trade fair. What to do?

Now, any reasonable person would say tough luck, lives are at stake and quarantine you must. But one of the cargo's owners was also the mayor of Marseille, so what do you think happened? Yup, the cargo was allowed to unload, with disastrous consequences—over 100,000 deaths, including half of Marseille.

As the plague worked its way north, the king and pope ordered a six-foot high stone wall to be built, nearly 20 miles long, with guard towers manned by soldiers. About four miles of the wall have been restored and there's a **walking path** that runs alongside it. You can reach it by starting at Parking Bourbourin† near Cabrières

---

\*    tinyurl.com/c7krhf9e

†    tinyurl.com/3tk2fwuz

d'Avignon. You can see the route on Google Maps\* (it takes about 15 minutes to get to the start of the wall.)

If you'd like to take a guided tour of the wall, Emily Durand of Your Private Provence† will be happy to organize one for you.

## Gordes and the Best Photo Spot

Gordes is one of the most popular hilltop villages in Provence. So much has been written about it that I don't have anything to add. I'll just point out two spots of special interest.

As you approach Gordes, the view of it is spectacular, with the village seeming to spill down the hillside. It makes you want to jump out of your car and take a picture. Unfortunately, so many people used to do that and stop traffic that the town finally built **a pull-off area where you can take photos**‡. It's so perfect that Instagram must have a zillion shots of people standing there with Gordes in the background.

For another nice view spot, some of the cafés in town have decks with wonderful views over the Luberon Valley. It's great to have a meal or drink and enjoy the view. My favorite is the back deck of Le Cercle Républicain§, on the Place du Château⸿ but others are good as well.

---

\*    tinyurl.com/3dk4xw2z

†    tinyurl.com/537a6kud

‡    tinyurl.com/3wjd4uph

§    tinyurl.com/5mtk544

⸿    tinyurl.com/azfu9bw

The Gordes tourist office[*] is at Place Genty Pantaly[†].

## Sénanque Abbey

This might be the most-photographed spot in Provence. If you've ever seen a picture of a lavender field in front of a lovely stone church, you've seen Sénanque Abbey[‡].

Built in the 12th century, it follows Cistercian precepts of a simple abbey without ornamentation—there are no frescoes inside, for example. But this simplicity gives it a special beauty and you should try to visit the inside of the abbey as well as admiring the outside.

Sénanque Abbey sits in a small wooded valley[§] below Gordes, giving it an especially beautiful location. Between late June and early August, when the lavender is in bloom, it is literally "picture postcard" perfect (it's on a lot of postcards.) It also attracts hordes of tourists, so **go early if you can**.

The abbey is still active and the monks sell lavender and honey products in their giftshop, as well as religious books and other gifts. If you walk down the path that leads behind the abbey, to where the monks live, you might see signs of their daily life—I remember once seeing a monk's shoes sitting on a windowsill, drying in the sun.

---

[*]    tinyurl.com/2ajjpk63
[†]    tinyurl.com/bxb5kanh
[‡]    tinyurl.com/4nw43x93
[§]    tinyurl.com/m25ydpkw

# The Bories Village

A borie is a small stone structure, built without mortar, that is similar to an Irish beehive hut. It is very striking looking. You see them here and there in Provence, sometimes falling apart, as most are hundreds of years old. They used to serve a lot of purposes—grain storage, tool shed, sheep shelter, small workshop, sometimes even a seasonal home.

If you'd like to learn more about them, there's an open-air museum a mile from Gordes called the Village des Bories[*] with about 20 bories in different shapes and sizes. It's definitely worth a short visit to see them. You might enjoy the Village des Bories website[†]—you can look at the photos and read the history, even if you don't go to the Village itself.

# A Riot of Color at Roussillon

If you love color, you'll love Roussillon[‡]. I go there every time I'm in Provence.

Imagine a cliff with bands of bright orange and yellow, and then bands of red and purple. You might think it's something out of a fairy tale but no, it's part of the natural landscape of Roussillon.

Roussillon was once the world capital of ochre, a naturally occurring pigment. It comes in an astonishing variety of

---

[*]   tinyurl.com/ykunem4y
[†]   tinyurl.com/ppb9zp7z
[‡]   tinyurl.com/y6cufll7

colors, from bright shades of yellow and orange to vivid red and purple. Ochre pigment is embedded in certain kinds of clay and was used as far back as prehistoric times, when cavemen used it for their paintings. It can be extracted to create dyes, and ochre mining was once a big business, with Roussillon its world center.

Eventually ochre mining died out but the quarries remain, and you can take the *Sentier des Ocres* (Ochre Path)[*][†] for an easy walk through the old quarries. The colors are magnificent! There are two routes, one that takes about 30 minutes and another that's about an hour, and both are magical.

Be warned however, that you will probably pick up **colorful dust on your shoes and pants**, so be prepared to brush it off. I once saw a white dog walking through the quarry with its owner. Well, it used to be white, because its legs and tummy were now bright orange.

Roussillon is a pleasant town, with cozy restaurants and a good viewing spot at the top of the village. If you would like to accompany your meal with a view of the colorful landscape, try Restaurant David at 1 Rue de la Poste[‡].

The town's tourist office[§] is at 19 Rue de la Poste[ꟗ].

---

[*]  tinyurl.com/yc3uu74j
[†]  tinyurl.com/aewvh3ny
[‡]  tinyurl.com/485d2ak5
[§]  tinyurl.com/3c5kam4z
[ꟗ]  tinyurl.com/2sezv9kx

If you haven't gotten your fill of ochre, be sure to check out the nearby **Colorado Provençal**[*] another area packed with ochre quarries.

For another view of ochre altogether, take a short drive[†] to the **Bruoux ochre mines**[‡*]. Here, instead of open-air quarries, ochre was mined by digging long tunnels into the hillsides, tunnels that are 30 feet high! There are miles and miles of these, forming a vast underground labyrinth, and a tour through them is both beautiful and fascinating[§].

## Bonnieux and a Fabulous Picnic Spot

Anchoring the east end of the Luberon Valley is the hilltop village of Bonnieux, with some of the best views around.

As you climb up into the village, you'll eventually come to the road called Cours Elzéar Pin (D36) with restaurant terraces along one side of it. They belong to La Terraza di Bonnieux[ſ**] and Val and I love to eat here. The food is fine but it's the view we come for, it's fantastic. The only downside is that you are right next to the road with cars going by—not a lot, but enough that you notice. There is also a rooftop bar and restaurant

---

[*] tinyurl.com/3apn5kdd
[†] tinyurl.com/263shmu7
[‡] tinyurl.com/4dzyhchc
[§] tinyurl.com/4s9sp9cs
[ſ] tinyurl.com/43hsn42c
[**] tinyurl.com/5uma79n4

across the street, Le Rooftop de Bonnieux*, which looks nice but we've never been.

For excellent food I go to Restaurant César,† just up the road.‡ It has a small menu with traditional dishes and I've had nothing but great meals here. Some of the tables have nice views—try to get one by a window.

If you love picnics, there's a great spot nearby with a fabulous view, even better than Bonnieux, **maybe my favorite view in Provence**. It's on the road to the *Fôret des Cedres* (Cedar Forest), a few miles outside of town.

To get there, take the D36 east towards Lourmarin, then turn right about a mile after you leave Bonnieux, onto the Chemin de la Fôret. Follow this up for about two miles until you see what looks like a wooden outhouse (it's not actually an outhouse, I don't know what it is.) There's a small parking area next to it§.

If you walk to the left from the parking area, through some trees, you'll find that fabulous view I promised you. Val and I like to spread a blanket under a tree and have a picnic here with our friends. The amazing thing is that you are looking *down* on Bonnieux, way down. When you realize how high up Bonnieux is, and that you are much higher, you understand why the view is so great.

---

\*    tinyurl.com/52ud4p3t
†    tinyurl.com/bddk6jjc
‡    tinyurl.com/3edyu6zk
§    tinyurl.com/3nbe97f3

You can continue on the road for about another mile and a half to the Cedar Forest*, which has some nice cool walks among the woods, but for me the best part is that view.

## Lacoste and a Favorite Café

Lacoste is a small hilltop village with only a few hundred residents, dominated by a ruined château† that once belonged to the infamous Marquis de Sade. It's now owned by Pierre Cardin, who is slowly restoring it.

Like a lot of hilltop villages, the views are great, especially from the château, which sits at the top of the village. The château also has some nice outdoor sculptures, and occasionally special events.

Lacoste also hosts the overseas campus of the Savannah College of Art and Design, so don't be surprised if you run into young people speaking English.

The reason I love Lacoste is the Café de France‡. It's a simple place with a wonderful view, perched on the side of a hill. You can enjoy your meal, or coffee, or glass of wine, and gaze across at Bonnieux, looking over orchards and vineyards and a couple of lavender fields. It's one of **my favorite places for a meal with a view**.

---

\*    tinyurl.com/469z2uds

†    tinyurl.com/r3eespv6

‡    tinyurl.com/8mw5rh8p

# True Farmer's Markets

Provence has dozens of wonderful outdoor markets, but only a few are run by the farmers themselves.

The little town of Coustellet holds one of these "producer's" markets[*] every Sunday morning. The locals shop there to stock up their kitchens, and with discerning customers like that you know it has to be good. Val and I often make a special trip there, and we are never disappointed.

The Coustellet market starts at 8am and ends at 1pm.

Another small town, Velleron, has an evening market[†] where farmers bring their produce fresh from the fields. They line up their trucks and sell fruits and vegetables right out of the back. The market is very popular because it's famous for having the best produce around.

The Velleron market opens at 6pm on Monday through Saturday during the summer season of April through September. Other times of the year it opens at 4:30pm on Tuesday, Friday, and Saturday.

# Lourmarin and a Michelin-Starred, Gluten-Free Restaurant

While it's not actually in the Luberon Valley, this is a gem of a village about 10 miles from Bonnieux via the D36.

---

[*]   tinyurl.com/ycvxcxvc

[†]   tinyurl.com/43jxvdk7

Lourmarin has **one of the best markets in Provence**, on Friday mornings, and an adorable little *centre ville*. It is also the final resting place of Albert Camus—lovers of French literature often visit his gravesite. This village is definitely worth a trip.

Lourmarin's tourist office[*] is at Place Henri Barthélémy[†].

## The World's Best Gluten-Free Restaurant

Right outside of Lourmarin is a great and unusual restaurant and hotel. Auberge la Fenière[‡][§] has had a Michelin star for decades, earned by Reine Sammut, one of France's leading chefs. A few years ago, she passed the reins to her daughter Nadia, who suffers from celiac disease, which means she absolutely cannot tolerate gluten (I'm the same.)

Nadia converted the menu to remove all gluten—a risky move. But she kept the Michelin star, making Fenière the world's only Michelin-starred and gluten-free restaurant. The food is spectacularly good, and the setting is gorgeous, making it a definite "special occasion" destination[¶].

In addition to the gastronomic restaurant, Fenière also has a casual bistro, and regularly offers cooking classes.

---

[*]    tinyurl.com/ywyakbb9
[†]    tinyurl.com/248xke6x   🌐
[‡]    tinyurl.com/2pehp42n
[§]    tinyurl.com/sjmu4urh   🌐
[¶]    tinyurl.com/u4j97x79

## Getting to Lourmarin

If you go to Lourmarin from Bonnieux (there are other routes), be aware that the road is winding, so it will take you about 20 minutes by car. If you want an interesting detour along the way, take the D943 to the Aiguebrun Valley, **a beautiful place that is well off the tourist track** and a nice place to hike. One good place to start is the Auberge des Seguins[*][†] near Buoux.

## More Info

For information about Lourmarin, my go-to source is Shutters and Sunflowers[‡], a terrific website run by a British-American woman who lives there part of the year.

## Ice Cream!

**If you are a fan of ice cream, sorbet, and wonderful views,** consider a drive to L'Art Glacier[§][ʃ] about 20 minutes east of Lourmarin. It's a little place with fabulous views over the Luberon. And the food! Their talented ice cream / sorbet maker offers about 50 flavors, from the usual suspects to flowers like rose and violet, fruits like cassis and ma khaen berry, and spices like cinnamon and Sichuan pepper. You can also get concoctions with

---

[*]  tinyurl.com/344f2a76
[†]  tinyurl.com/hy9778f
[‡]  tinyurl.com/pzryxpy9
[§]  tinyurl.com/na2w8wrm
[ʃ]  tinyurl.com/e59tpjw

whipped cream and nuts and such, but I recommend the straight flavors.

## An Easy Bike Route

One of my favorite biking routes is the Véloroute du Calavon[*], which runs up the Luberon Valley. It's a pretty ride and **very, very easy**.

You can see the route on Google Maps[†].

This is a *voie verte*, or "greenway," a paved route for bikers, walkers and rollerbladers. There is a network of them in France, many built where railroad tracks used to be, which makes them nice and flat.

The Véloroute du Calavon begins in Cavaillon and goes to Apt, though it is not yet complete so there are gaps along the way[‡].

Val and I like to start near the village of Baumettes. To get there, we take the D900 and get off at the D29 exit going south. After about 200 yards there is a small parking lot on the left[§] and we join the Véloroute from there.

We head east, with a rocky hillside on our left and the valley floor on our right. After a couple of miles, we pass the abandoned Goult train station[¶], which looks a

---

[*]   tinyurl.com/5praz7h5
[†]   tinyurl.com/cpz52hnx
[‡]   tinyurl.com/55c3hxnr
[§]   tinyurl.com/dd9ff2y4
[¶]   tinyurl.com/5554x8mt

bit forlorn sitting next to where the train tracks used to be. Nearby is a bathroom if the need arises.

A few hundred yards later, and just off to the right, we like to stop and look at the Dolmen de l'Ubac* a large megalithic tomb. It was only discovered in 1995, after the Calavon River flooded and revealed its location. There is a sign with information about the dolmen (in French) right next to the véloroute, plus a path down to it.

After another four miles, we reach Pont Julien†, a Roman bridge that crosses the Calavon. It was built 2,000 years ago and looks solid enough to go a couple of thousand more. It was still used for auto traffic until a few years ago!

The bridge is very picturesque and we sometimes stop to have a picnic lunch on the riverbank before heading back to Baumettes. Or we detour off of the Véloroute onto the D106, partway between Baumettes and Pont Julien, and puff our way up to Lacoste to eat at the Café de France‡. It has fabulous views over the Luberon Valley, and after lunch we hop on our bikes and coast all the way back to the Véloroute.

---

\*    tinyurl.com/2dp2avuz

†    tinyurl.com/4zm8sc8w

‡    tinyurl.com/8mw5rh8p

# The Rhône Valley Wine Region

The Rhône Valley is one of France's largest and best wine regions, stretching over 100 miles from Vienne down almost to the Mediterranean Sea. The southern part of the Rhône Valley, which is in and near Provence, produces richly flavored wines, reflecting the warm weather that attracts so many of us.

For my money, the wines of the southern Rhône are the best values around. Let me tell you about some of my favorite spots, but you can go almost anywhere and you won't be disappointed.

## Châteauneuf-du-Pape, the Town That Banned UFOs

This is the where you'll find some of the top wines in France. The name of the town means "new château of the pope" because the popes of Avignon built a summer palace here. And popes need good wine to drink so vineyards were planted, and the rest is history.

If you look at the vineyards surrounding Châteauneuf-du-Pape, you'll notice that many of them are covered with big, round stones. These *galets roulés* are one of the secrets to the wines' deliciousness—they absorb heat during the day and reflect it back to the vines during the night, helping the grapes ripen.

Here are some my favorite things to do in Châteauneuf-du-Pape, though the town is so pretty and inviting that you can't go wrong just strolling around on your own.

The Châteauneuf-du-Pape tourist office* is at 3 Rue de la République†.

---

*     tinyurl.com/2jem4fa3
†     tinyurl.com/3d6v55k5

## The Pope's Château

The famous château is now a ruin, but what's left still dominates the town*. The best part is the view from the château, with vineyards spreading out in all directions, like green velvet covering the hills and valleys.

## Le Verger des Papes Restaurant and Wine Cellar

This combination restaurant and wine cellar is only a few steps from the pope's château, with excellent food, wine, and (especially) views. I recommend starting with the wine cellar, which is built into the hillside†. They have a nice variety of Châteauneuf-du-Pape wines so you can compare different wineries.

Right next to it is the restaurant‡ § with very good food and extraordinary views. **Get a table on the terrace** and gaze out over the vineyards while you enjoy your meal. With wine, of course. Go ahead, have another glass.

## A Favorite Winery

A few years ago, Val and I had the opportunity to meet Françoise Roumieux, the owner and winemaker of Clos du Calvaireᶴ. We were introduced by my French

---

\*   tinyurl.com/27xtyyuk

†   tinyurl.com/34hsnjzc

‡   tinyurl.com/3t775knp

§   tinyurl.com/7xam6r2e

ᶴ   tinyurl.com/bdd63bay

doctor after I broke my wrist in a bike accident—it's a funny story* (the introduction, not the broken wrist.) Françoise gave us a tour and tasting and we discovered how delicious her wines are. Clos du Calvaire's beautiful tasting room† is a two-minute walk from the tourist office and is a great way to start or end a visit to Châteauneuf-du-Pape.

## The World's Greatest Wine Tasting?

Every year in April, the town holds what must be the **greatest wine tasting ever‡**. The Salon des Vins brings together all of the town's winemakers, about 100 of them, in the municipal recreation center. They stand behind fold-up tables topped with bottles of their wine, ready to share them with you. It's an informal affair with not a wine snob in sight, and **it costs only 10 euro** to enter (I repeat, 10 euro!) You can taste all the wine you want—you just walk up to a winemaker, put out your glass, and ask for a pour. If you like it, you can buy a bottle right there.

When it's time for lunch, there are food vendors from all over France, selling their delicacies in a courtyard outside, plus tables where you can sit and enjoy them.

---

\*    tinyurl.com/y7ognvsw

†    tinyurl.com/65kwfz4w

‡    tinyurl.com/kha46ypv

## The Flying Saucer Law

Back in the 1950s, the movie *The War of the Worlds* came out and a UFO craze swept France. Citizens all over the country started reporting seeing flying saucers (also called "flying cigars" in French.) The mayor of Châteauneuf-du-Pape saw an opportunity for some free publicity and quickly passed a law banning UFOs*. As he had hoped, journalists from around the world descended on the town, wanting to know the whys and wherefores and writing breathless articles, which led to a burst of tourism.

Surprisingly (or maybe not), the law is still on the books. Asked why, a recent mayor noted that "it spices things up a bit." And, as anyone in town will tell you, the law works—no UFOs have landed for decades!

# Gigondas, Wine Village with a View

With wines similar to those of Châteauneuf-du-Pape, but with **much lower prices**, I find myself buying a frightening amount of wine from Gigondas. It's a good thing my French friends help me drink it.

The village is perched on a mountainside, overlooking the vineyards that bring it fame. Above it are the jagged, rocky crests of the Dentelles de Montmirail, a small mountain range. Even in a region known for its natural beauty, Gigondas stands out.

---

\*    tinyurl.com/uyngzkz

Gigondas makes wine tasting easy at the Caveau du Gigondas[*] at 9 Place Gabrielle Andéol[†], a tasting room that offers the wines of many of the village's winemakers all in one place. Sip, savor, compare, and then pick up a few bottles. My personal favorite is Notre Dame des Pallières[‡], an under-the-radar producer of excellent wines, with a friendly tasting room at 311 Route de Lencieux[§] a few miles north of town.

Also in the center of town, near the Caveau du Gigondas, are two restaurants I like a lot. If you prefer a casual meal, I recommend Du Verre à l'Assiette[¶] on the Place du Portail[**] with good food and reasonable prices. They have comfortable outdoor seating and there's nothing like a leisurely lunch under leafy trees on a warm summer day.

For gastronomic fare, l'Oustalet[††] at 5 Place Gabrielle Andèol[‡‡] is the place to go. Holder of a coveted Michelin star, it attracts foodies from all over. Be sure to **make your reservations early!**

There's nothing like biking through French vineyards, so consider renting a bike and exploring the surrounding countryside. While I haven't used them, Veloz[§§] electric bike rental in nearby Sablet is highly rated. Don't miss

---

[*]     tinyurl.com/ydc977zs
[†]     tinyurl.com/4322r2wb
[‡]     tinyurl.com/86e24abd
[§]     tinyurl.com/h6wjnhmb
[¶]     tinyurl.com/3sstr7ab
[**]    tinyurl.com/42zk5pu8
[††]    tinyurl.com/48xrjbhy
[‡‡]    tinyurl.com/my795nna
[§§]    tinyurl.com/beav5zbb

the village of Séguret*, four miles away and one of the Most Beautiful Villages of France†. Six miles further is Vaison-la-Romaine‡, a lovely town with some of the best Roman ruins in France.

If you are feeling energetic, there is **a hiking path above Gigondas with fabulous views**. To get there, as you are going up the D80 towards Gigondas, don't turn right into town but instead follow the signs for Dentelles de Montmirail. After a few minutes you will reach the Parking les Floréts§. From here, it's a steep 15-minute walk to the trail, with some beautiful views along the way. At the top you turn right and enjoy the views as you go (this part is mostly flat.)

After about a mile you'll see some picnic tables on your right and a stairway climbing through the trees. This is another steep climb, about 5 minutes, at which point you will come to a viewing platform. It has an orientation table that allows you to identify what you are seeing. The views are magnificent! Some of the route up is rocky, so sturdy shoes are recommended. I usually turn around here, but the trail goes on for miles, with more beautiful scenery to enjoy.

The Gigondas tourist office¶ is at 5 Rue du Portail**.

---

\*    tinyurl.com/3h5sdef7
†    tinyurl.com/a6ujnb52
‡    tinyurl.com/s3hfe9d7
§    tinyurl.com/3kkd4m65
¶    tinyurl.com/5vzf7yzd
\*\* tinyurl.com/2xuvubtk

# Aix-en-Provence

Aix has plenty of interesting sights, but the best part of the town is just hanging out.

Part of Aix's ambience is due to it being a college town. There are three universities in Aix and students make up a quarter of the city's population, so there are lots of lively cafés, bars, and restaurants. My favorite thing to do is walk around the old part of town, between the

Cours Mirabeau and city hall (*Hôtel de Ville*), to see what looks interesting.

Aix's tourist office[*] is at 300 Avenue Giuseppe Verdi[†].

# Parking

Aix has lots of parking lots but I think some are leftovers from the Dark Ages. They are cramped and gloomy, and you are lucky if you escape without scraping your car on a wall or a post.

**The best place to park** is in the Parking Rotonde[‡] right in the middle of town. This underground lot is big and well-lit and has indicators showing where the empty spaces are. You take an elevator to exit after you've parked, and the place where you get out is also where you pay your ticket when you return. The Parking Rotonde is conveniently located next to the tourist office, so it's a good place to start your visit.

# Cours Mirabeau

This is a broad, tree-lined boulevard[§] with wide sidewalks and lots of cafés and restaurants. It's **one of the best people-watching spots in France**—just take a seat, have a drink, and watch the world go by. The most famous café,

---

[*]   tinyurl.com/6k78bu5m
[†]   tinyurl.com/6exb9xbc
[‡]   tinyurl.com/5e7wpx65
[§]   tinyurl.com/yttzyhfz

until it burned down under mysterious circumstances, was Les Deux Garcons, a hangout of artists like Cézanne and Picasso. In another sad turn, some of the trees along the Cours Mirabeau have been felled by disease in recent years. But it is still the heart of Aix!

## Markets

If you love markets, you are in luck, because **Aix has a market every day**, and sometimes two.

The daily food market is in the Place Richelme[*] a beautiful square near the town hall. It is a comfortable place to have a meal or a drink after the market clears out.

Three days a week (Tuesday, Thursday, Saturday) the market expands to include crafts, clothing, and everything else you expect in a Provençal market. It spreads all over town, with one of the best parts on the Cours Mirabeau.

Almost every day there is a flower market in the Place de l'Hôtel de Ville[†]. This square is already pretty but all those flowers make it even prettier.

## Art

Aix's most famous son is the painter Paul Cézanne, considered the founder of modern art. Among his many works, he painted the mountain that looms over

---

[*]   tinyurl.com/7uamdjzw
[†]   tinyurl.com/4sascu7x

the city, Mont Sainte-Victoire, dozens of times. Today you can visit his art studio, the Atelier Cézanne* at 9 Avenue Paul Cézanne† which remains much as he left it.

If you'd like to visit a museum, there are two excellent ones in Aix, the Hôtel de Caumont art center‡ at 3 rue Joseph Cabassol§ and the Musée Granet⁋ at Place Saint Jean de Malte**.

## Santons

One of the best shops for these beloved figurines is Santons Fouque†† at 65 Cours Gambetta‡‡. The family that owns it has been making award-winning santons since 1934 and the company is now run by the fourth generation of santon makers.

---

* tinyurl.com/dcur33ac
† tinyurl.com/byn2v7h9
‡ tinyurl.com/x9wux47c
§ tinyurl.com/ufmvuyjh
⁋ tinyurl.com/ef82j2wb
** tinyurl.com/yrjpvtmf
†† tinyurl.com/vheuf8x5
‡‡ tinyurl.com/cjabe3xw

## Cheese!

If you love cheese, stop by La Fromagerie du Passage[*]. Located in the Passage Agard[†] just off the Cours Mirabeau, it not only has a great selection of cheese, but also a restaurant upstairs with a sunny terrace.

## Hiking

My favorite hiking trail near Aix is a six-mile loop that starts near the Bimont Dam (*Barrage de Bimont.*) It's along the side of Mont Sainte-Victoire, with excellent views as you go, including Zola Dam and Zola Lake (the father of author Émile Zola designed the dam.) There is an online map of the trail[‡] that shows the starting point on the western side. I prefer to start at the eastern end, at the Bimont Dam parking lot[§].

On the way to the trail, you'll pass Vauvenargue and its famous château[¶]. The château was once owned by Pablo Picasso and he is buried there. It's not open to visitors but the view of the château from the town, and the of mountainside behind it, is gorgeous.

---

[*]   tinyurl.com/ahvjapw4
[†]   tinyurl.com/attrhk2z
[‡]   tinyurl.com/awpjdju3
[§]   tinyurl.com/bmju49m6
[¶]   tinyurl.com/y2axajmr

# Further Afield

## The Cave of Forgotten Dreams

You may have seen photos of the stunning prehistoric cave paintings in Lascaux. Well, if you'd like to see paintings that are **even older and just as remarkable**, head to the Chauvet Cave (Grotte Chauvet.)[*] It is an amazing place about an hour north of Avignon, near one of France's most spectacular canyons.

Lascaux created a sensation when it was discovered in 1940. Thousands flocked to see its famous pot-bellied horses—so many, in fact, that the paintings started to deteriorate. Eventually the French government created the imitation cave that tourists visit today.

When the Chauvet Cave was discovered in 1994, the government decided to avoid its earlier mistake, so the cave was sealed off from all but a few scientists and artists. Werner Herzog's 2010 documentary, Cave of

---

[*]   tinyurl.com/lroh2so

Forgotten Dreams*, gave the world a glimpse of these ancient wonders.

In 2015 a new museum complex opened†, called the Grotte Chauvet 2, that recreates the Chauvet Cave and its glories. The museum is at the end of the Gorge d'Ardeche‡, a steep, winding canyon created by the waters of the Ardeche River.

If you are daring, you can reach the museum by taking the narrow D290 road that is cut into the edge of the canyon. It features 800-foot sheer drops and no guardrails—my palms still sweat when I remember driving it! The views are spectacular but you might prefer the more sedate route along the D4.

The paintings in the Chauvet Cave are the oldest in the world, dating back 36,000 years—back when Homo Sapiens and Neanderthals were still duking it out. They depict animals that no longer exist in Europe, like **buffalo, lions and rhinos.**

The museum not only recreates the paintings but also the entire cave, including stalagmites and stalactites and the animal bones on the ground—the semi-circle of bear skulls is especially striking. Guided tours run throughout the day and **booking ahead is strongly advised.**

The adjoining museum explains the history of the cave, the region, and humanity's development in Europe. It has full-sized re-creations of some of the animals that

---

\*     tinyurl.com/rp5mtkp8

†     tinyurl.com/3jdwv2ec

‡     tinyurl.com/2jcyf25w

were painted, like wholly rhinos. And there are "ask the scientist" kiosks where famous scientists answer questions via video recordings.

Nearby is the Pont d'Arc* a natural limestone arch that crosses the Ardeche River. It's a natural wonder and fun to kayak under[†].

## Prehistoric Art in Marseille

In 1991, Henri Cosquer made a remarkable discovery[‡]: he found a grotto filled with prehistoric paintings. Even more remarkable is that the cave is only accessible via an underwater passageway.

Cosquer was a professional diver who led underwater tours near Marseille. In his spare time, he liked to explore the nooks and crannies of the rugged coastline.

One day, Cosquer noticed an underwater passageway that he decided to investigate. It led to a web of tunnels that took many dives to explore, until one day he surfaced inside a cave filled with stalagmites and stalactites.

As Cosquer swam through it, he was stunned to find a human handprint on a wall, then paintings of animals. He realized that he had stumbled onto a set of prehistoric cave paintings, lost to the world for thousands of years. What is today an underwater passageway was once

---

\*   tinyurl.com/f8b7t57u

†   tinyurl.com/c7rccmdf

‡   tinyurl.com/mrax6f9k

above ground, back when sea levels were lower during the Ice Age.

The French have now built a replica[*] of this cave in Marseille, near the Old Port[†]. Because the real cave is partly filled with water, today's visitors travel through its replica on small electric vehicles. It is highly realistic, with stalagmites and paintings throughout. And some of the animal paintings are surprising, like the penguins, who once swam in the Mediterranean when the climate was much colder!

## The Underwater Museum of Marseille

You usually find statues in places like museums, cathedrals, and sculpture gardens. And now visitors to Marseille can enjoy them in a new location—underwater.

The Underwater Museum of Marseille (*Musée Subaquatique de Marseille*)[‡] opened its doors, so to speak, in 2020 with ten newly-created sculptures near a popular city beach called Les Catalans[§]. Admission is free, and guided tours are also available.

The statues are made of a type of concrete that attracts sea life, both flora and fauna, creating a kind of artificial

---

[*]   tinyurl.com/y3njtw6c
[†]   tinyurl.com/2npba5yk  
[‡]   tinyurl.com/75nvzk8j
[§]   tinyurl.com/2ddwbc8a

reef. One starfish took up residence only days after a statue was installed[*]!

Statues include the sea god Poseidon (of course), plus sea nymphs, giant animals, and my favorite, the haunting The Seed and the Sea[†].

The Underwater Museum has artistic and scientific missions and is an excellent site for studying the Mediterranean's underwater biosphere. It has established partnerships with local schools, using the new attraction to educate students about marine conservation.

The museum is located about 100 yards offshore from the city center beach Les Catalans and is ringed by a circle of security buoys to make it easy to find. The sculptures are 15 feet underwater and easily accessible to swimmers (masks recommended).

The museum has attracted a lot of press, and was featured on the popular French television show Thalassa[‡].

## Cassis and the Fjords of France

East of Marseille lies the sparkling little coastal town of **Cassis**, nestled at the bottom of steep, vineyard-covered hills that come almost to the sea. It's so adorably cute that you might think you are walking into the Provence World section of Disneyland, if there were

---

[*]   tinyurl.com/2xp4j68v

[†]   tinyurl.com/tvy79fzj

[‡]   tinyurl.com/x2m98e92

such a thing. There's nothing better than a stroll through town followed by a bowl of fish soup or some *moules-frites* at one of the restaurants that line the docks.

The setting of Cassis is dramatic, with Cap Canaille—the highest cliff in France—towering over the town to the east. And to the west are the beautiful and rugged calanques, the so-called fjords of France[*].

These stunning geologic features make up the Calanques National Park, which stretches between Marseille and Cassis. Dominated by stark grey limestone and dabbed with greenery here and there, the park provides a sharp contrast to the deep blue waters of the Mediterranean Sea. Eons ago, rivers carved canyons through this limestone on their way to the sea, forming the calanques we see today.

**The easiest way to see them is by boat**. You can choose from a variety of different rides lasting from 45 minutes to two hours, which cover as few as three or as many as nine calanques. The ticket office is at the Quai Saint-Pierre in Cassis[†] but be aware that seats sell out in the high season so you should **get there early**.

Adventurous visitors might choose to **hike to the calanques.** The one closest to Cassis is about a 30-minute walk away, but you can continue on and go as far as your legs will take you. The trails are uneven and steep in parts, so be sure to wear solid footgear and carry plenty of water. **Note:** this route has become so popular that

---

[*]   tinyurl.com/y55b9f4w
[†]   tinyurl.com/d3ztzmay

access is sometimes restricted. Be sure to check at the tourist office before heading out.

Also consider the drive from Cassis to La Ciotat, called the Route des Crêtes. The D141 road runs along the cliff top joining the two towns—it's a 10-mile drive that takes about 30 minutes. The views are stunning and there are plenty of photo-ops along the way. A word of caution: this road is subject to occasional closure on days where there is an elevated fire risk or extreme wind. You can call +33 (0)8 11 20 13 13 to verify that the Route des Crêtes is open.

The Cassis tourist office[*] is at Quai des Moulins[†].

# Nice and the Most Russian Spot in France

The city of Nice is famous for a lot of things, like its Old Town and the Marc Chagall Museum. And let's not forget the Promenade des Anglais with those famous blue chairs[‡]! But did you know that Nice is also home to the most Russian spot in France?

Yes, the Saint Nicholas Orthodox Cathedral was built in 1912 in memory of Nicholas Alexandrovich, the one-time heir to the Russian throne who died in Nice. It was designed in the classic style, with five beautiful onion domes. Seeing the cathedral, you think you've

---

[*]    tinyurl.com/rvnekt5u
[†]    tinyurl.com/3vzn4mps
[‡]    tinyurl.com/5bed65ds

somehow stumbled into Moscow! Today it is a National Monument of France and one of the most visited sites of the French Riviera[*].

The cathedral fell into disrepair over the years but has recently been restored to its former glory. You can admire its rich decorations, with many paintings, frescos, icons and other intricate details[†].

The cathedral[‡] is located on Avenue Nicolas II[§].

The Nice tourist office[¶] is on Avenue Thiers[**].

## Eating in Nice

Nice is a foodie paradise, due to its seaside location and its access to the bounty of Provence. Like many French cities, it has its specialties and here are a few of my favorites[††].

### Salade Niçoise

No trip to Nice, or France for that matter, is complete without a salade niçoise. You get to choose which version you want because this is a dish with many variations. The original salad, served in Nice over a century ago, was a

---

[*]   tinyurl.com/y5o6r9tk
[†]   tinyurl.com/3sbyek5p
[‡]   tinyurl.com/33u3m6ht
[§]   tinyurl.com/a682sec
[¶]   tinyurl.com/y4dbfm48
[**]  tinyurl.com/3zrxduza
[††]  tinyurl.com/yagrep5a

simple combination of tomatoes, anchovies and olive oil. Over the years, other ingredients have been added, like tuna, hard-boiled eggs, potatoes and green beans. Today there are as many variations as there are chefs. Would you like corn? Olives? Seared ahi tuna? Take your pick!

## Pan Bagnat

The *pan bagnat* sandwich, popular in Nice, is like a *salade niçoise* between two slices of bread. To make it, take a *boule* or other round loaf, cut it in half top and bottom, and drizzle each piece with olive oil. And by drizzle, I mean pour it on because you really can't have too much good olive oil! Then layer on hard-boiled egg, tuna, anchovies, tomato, onion, cucumber and more. You can stop there, knowing that it will be messy to eat, or do as the good people of Nice do—squish it together tightly and store it in the fridge for a few hours so it holds together better.

## Ratatouille

This Provençal favorite originated in Nice, where it is sometimes called ratatouille niçoise. It's a stewed vegetable dish, typically made with tomatoes, eggplant, zucchini, onions and garlic, though there are many variations of this dish. Some chefs cook all the vegetables together from the start, but purists insist they be cooked separately and then combined at the end. Like a lot of stews, ratatouille improves if you keep it in the refrigerator overnight and then eat it the next day.

## Pissaladière

This dish has a crust like a pizza, but it's square instead of round and there's no cheese or sauce. Instead, a pissaladière is topped with caramelized onions, black olives and anchovies. The name comes from the old Ligurian word for "salted fish."

## Socca

Socca is a flatbread made from a simple batter of chickpea flour, olive oil, and water. This is cooked into a kind of big crêpe and then cut into triangular slices, drizzled with olive oil and sprinkled with sea salt. Eat it warm, when it's at its best. The dish originated in Genoa and is called *farinata* in Italian. People are so passionate about socca that one fellow even made a fun movie* about it!

---

* tinyurl.com/4x7fvv36

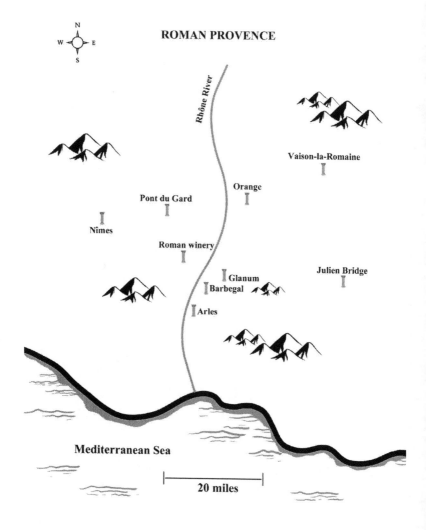

ROMAN PROVENCE

N
W · E
S

Rhône River

Vaison-la-Romaine

Orange

Pont du Gard

Nîmes

Roman winery

Glanum

Barbegal

Julien Bridge

Arles

Mediterranean Sea

20 miles

# Roman Provence

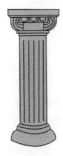

Way back around 50 B.C., Julius Caesar conquered Gaul (now France) and the area remained part of the Roman Empire for centuries. Today there are Roman ruins all over France, but the best are in and around Provence. In fact, 'Provence' comes from the Latin 'Provincia Romana,' the name of the large Roman province along the Mediterranean coast.

For history buffs, or anyone who would like to see some amazing sights, Provence is a wonderland.

# Highlights

- *The triple-decker Pont du Gard aqueduct is* **one of the top sights in all of France.** *It spans a wide valley and is as tall as an 18-story building*

- *The Maison Carrée in Nîmes is considered* **the world's most perfect Roman temple**

- **Dress like a Roman** *(virtually) in Nîme's Roman history museum. Hey, you look good in that toga!*

- *If you want to see a* **beautiful Roman arena,** *you have your pick from Nîmes and Arles, both of which have arenas that are still in use.*

- *See the* **hundred-foot-long Roman ship** *recovered from the bottom of the Rhône River*

- *Taste some* **Roman-style wine**—*not your usual glass of Chardonnay!*

# Where to Go: Arles or Nîmes?

If you have a limited appetite for Roman history, you might want to visit either Nîmes or Arles but not both, as their major sights are similar. Each has a large and well-preserved arena and an excellent Roman history museum. Nîmes gets extra points for its magnificent temple and imposing guard tower, while Arles scores for its theater and ancient burial grounds. Nîmes might get the nod because it is near the magnificent Pont du

Gard aqueduct, but Arles has van Gogh and who doesn't love ol' Vincent?

The choice is yours, but if you have limited time, you might want to pick just one of these fascinating cities.

# Arles

Arles sits on the banks of the mighty Rhône River, which made it the perfect hub for Roman sea and river trade. Large ships that plied the waters of the Mediterranean Sea would come to Arles to exchange cargo with the smaller vessels that could navigate the Rhône, or would unpack their loads for overland travel to other cities in the empire.

With all of this coming-and-going, it was inevitable that some of the cargo would slip overboard, presumably lost forever. But in recent years scientists have been able to explore the river's murky depths and have made some **remarkable discoveries**. First was the bust of Julius Caesar[*], considered the best ever found. Then came an actual Roman barge over 100 feet long. Both are now in the Museum of Ancient Arles[†][‡] along with mosaics, coins, and other artifacts from the glory days of the empire[§].

---

[*]    tinyurl.com/54854d2j
[†]    tinyurl.com/rpx2uwcn
[‡]    tinyurl.com/33hvfb2v
[§]    tinyurl.com/y5ts43r5

The centerpiece of Roman Arles is its 15,000-seat arena[*], recently cleaned and still used for concerts and outdoor sports. Nearby is a Roman theater that was buried for centuries and only rediscovered in the 19th century. There is also a sprawling Roman burial ground called the Alyscamps[†] that you can explore for hours.

## Van Gogh in Arles

Vincent van Gogh spent over a year in Arles, before that unfortunate business with his ear sent him to St-Rémy's mental asylum. You can take a walking tour[‡] through Arles to see many of the places where he painted. My favorite is the location of his painting *Café Terrace at Night*. The café is still in business, now called the Le Café van Gogh, in the Place du Forum[§] which is a nice square with lots of cafés.

## Also in Arles

Stop by the Romanesque St-Trophime church[ſ] and admire the fabulous carvings over the main entrance. Next door is the entrance to the beautiful cloisters.

The LUMA Foundation[**][††] is an art center housed in a building designed by the famous architect Frank Gehry[‡‡].

---

[*]    tinyurl.com/ebp4ahx5
[†]    tinyurl.com/4kr5r6tu
[‡]    tinyurl.com/2j4acwr2
[§]    tinyurl.com/mpwkana5
[ſ]    tinyurl.com/56w986nx
[**]   tinyurl.com/pe3puywz
[††]   tinyurl.com/y6y3srtd
[‡‡]   tinyurl.com/f4j4dhkw

He's best known for the Guggenheim Museum in Bilbao, and the LUMA building's crazy tower takes things to another level.

For another dramatic building, check out the Villa Benkemoun[*][†] which epitomizes groovy 1970s architecture. Designed by a disciple of Le Corbusier, it's a curvy, swirling masterpiece, complete with distinctive 70s furniture, that's been recognized as a national treasure of France. It's not always open so you'll need to contact them ahead of time to organize a tour.

## Dining

Place du Forum is a big, shady square full of restaurants and cafés, watched over by a towering statue of the Provençal writer Frédéric Mistral. Along one side is the Café Van Gogh, which inspired Vincent's famous painting *Café Terrace at Night*. The square is a lively spot for a meal, but my favorite place to eat is La Gueule du Loup[‡], just steps away at 39 Rue des Arènes[§].

The Arles tourist office[⁋] is at 9 Boulevard des Lices[**].

---

[*] tinyurl.com/y3nsz7e7
[†] tinyurl.com/68mhm7bs
[‡] tinyurl.com/349x7p49
[§] tinyurl.com/2sz8vkur
[⁋] tinyurl.com/2bernhtt
[**] tinyurl.com/ubuvak2r

# Nîmes

Nîmes was the capital of Provincia Romana, though it is not in present-day Provence. Once known as "the most Roman city outside of Italy," at its heart is a 24,000-seat Roman arena[*]. It is one of the largest and best-preserved in the world and is still in use today, for events ranging from concerts to mock gladiator battles.

Nearby is the Maison Carrée[†] perhaps the world's most perfect Roman temple. It has been cleaned in recent years and is sparkling white, like back in Roman times. Further on is the Tour Magne[‡], a massive tower that was once part of the city's fortifications.

Tying it all together is the recently-opened Roman history museum[§][ꝼ] across the street from the arena. It has some of the **best Roman mosaics outside of Pompeii**, as well as many interactive displays that are fun for the kids and bring the ancient city to life[**]—be sure to check out the one that lets you "dress like a Roman."

On the second floor of the museum is an excellent place for lunch, La Table du 2[††], with an outstanding view of the Roman arena across the street.

The town's tourist office[‡‡] is at 6 Boulevard des Arènes[§§].

---

| | |
|---|---|
| [*] | tinyurl.com/ys495nxp  |
| [†] | tinyurl.com/4hv52hst |
| [‡] | tinyurl.com/y7cnc7kc |
| [§] | tinyurl.com/xxxzbnjk |
| [ꝼ] | tinyurl.com/272xjmt7 |
| [**] | tinyurl.com/yxve7bg2 |
| [††] | tinyurl.com/e6vxjd4f |
| [‡‡] | tinyurl.com/wtkzet45 |
| [§§] | tinyurl.com/akhbj8nu  |

# The Stunning Pont du Gard Aqueduct

Ancient Nîmes had an elaborate system of fountains and public baths that required a steady supply of water. The closest major spring was many miles away, so Roman engineers built a gigantic system of canals and pipes to bring its waters to town. One of the challenges was crossing the Gardon River Valley, which cut right across their path. No problem! The Romans built an aqueduct to cross the valley, the Pont du Gard*† and it's enormous: as tall as the Statue of Liberty's torch and long enough to park three jumbo jets.

To make it so tall, the engineers came up with an elegant three-tier design: huge base arches are topped by progressively smaller ones. Gazing up at it is **awe-inspiring**!

Next to the Pont du Gard is an excellent museum that explains the whole water system and how the Romans built it. Nearby is a casual bistro, Les Petites Terraces, with an excellent view of the Pont. Not far away, on the other side of the river, is an even nicer restaurant, Les Terraces, also with an excellent view of the Pont.

For a cool excursion on a hot day, consider a kayak trip down the Gardon River‡, floating under the Pont du Gard itself.

---

*     tinyurl.com/4ju4sc6x
†     tinyurl.com/2hzwz5xj
‡     tinyurl.com/cx82mptr

Near the Pont is the beautiful town of Uzès, with one of the best central squares in France and a bustling Saturday-morning market. If you are thinking of visiting, which I highly recommend, the website Barefoot Blogger[*] is a great source of information.

Also near Pont du Gard is **one of my favorite wineries**, a source for inexpensive but delicious wines that's also near a great picnic spot[†].

# Other Roman Sites

## Orange

Orange is best-known for its magnificent Roman theater[‡], and performers come from all over the world for its annual summer festival. The main wall of the theater is over 120 feet tall and is so stunning that King Louis XIV called it, "the most beautiful wall in my kingdom."

Orange also boasts a Roman triumphal arch that's a bit like the Arc de Triomphe in Paris, and there's an excellent museum of Roman art and history.

The Orange tourist office[§] is at 5 Cours Aristide Briand[¶].

---

[*] tinyurl.com/3bd78pad
[†] tinyurl.com/vekpnv7k
[‡] tinyurl.com/48sbnj4w
[§] tinyurl.com/fdy4btcc
[¶] tinyurl.com/wwv2au23

## Vaison-la-Romaine

Further north from Orange, Vaison-la-Romaine boasts the ruins of a Roman town, an ancient Roman bridge, and a well-preserved Roman theater. Vaison is unusual in the way the Roman, medieval, and modern towns—together spanning over 2,000 years of history—lie so close together.

The Vaison tourist office[*] is at 5 Avenue Général de Gaulle[†].

## Glanum

St-Rémy-de-Provence began as the settlement of Glanum. The ruins of this important Roman city have been excavated and it is well worth a visit to see the remains of its temples, baths, markets, and houses. Right across the road are a well-preserved triumphal arch and a mausoleum, standing side by side.

See the St-Rémy-de-Provence section for more information about Glanum.

## The Greatest Power of the Ancient World

Near Fontvieille[‡] are the remains of a Roman aqueduct, part of an elaborate system that once brought water to Arles. Water would travel through the aqueduct and then have to go down a steep, rocky hillside to continue

---

[*]   tinyurl.com/45a6ssbj

[†]   tinyurl.com/83ywnc5k

[‡]   tinyurl.com/rucdavue

its journey. "Why not take advantage of this?" thought the clever Romans.

Their engineers designed a series of mills* that the water raced through, one after another, as it tumbled down the hillside. The power they generated could mill grain for 12,000 people a day! Historians call it, "**the greatest concentration of mechanical power in the ancient world**." You can see a mockup of it in the Museum of Ancient Arles†.

## The Julien Bridge

Near Bonnieux in the Luberon Valley is Pont Julien‡, a Roman bridge that crosses the Calavon River. It was built 2,000 years ago and is so solid it was still used for auto traffic until a few years ago! It's very picturesque and we sometimes have a picnic lunch on the riverbank next to it.

## The Roman Winery

One of the most interesting wineries in Provence§ is the Mas des Tourelles¶** near Beaucaire. Once a Roman villa, then a winery of great renown, part of it has now been made into an authentic Roman vineyard and winery.

---

*    tinyurl.com/hbwfju7e
†    tinyurl.com/rpx2uwcn
‡    tinyurl.com/4zm8sc8w  
§    tinyurl.com/2mz2vzdj
¶    tinyurl.com/ywzcfek4
**  tinyurl.com/ytsrczfe

You can take a tour, see a video on Roman winemaking techniques, then taste wines made using ancient Roman recipes. Some are sweet and pleasant, with honey used as an ingredient. Others are, shall we say, "interesting." Fenugreek in your wine, anyone?

Mas des Tourelles makes for an interesting stop for lovers of history and of wine alike. There is grape juice for the kids and a room full of Roman games they can play.

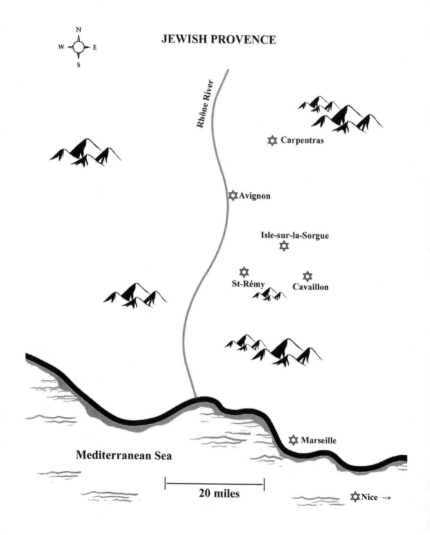

**JEWISH PROVENCE**

Rhône River

Carpentras

Avignon

Isle-sur-la-Sorgue

St-Rémy    Cavaillon

Marseille

Mediterranean Sea

20 miles

Nice →

# Jewish Provence

**People are often surprised to learn that France has the third-largest Jewish population in the world, after Israel and the United States.**

And they are even more surprised to learn that for centuries **the center of Jewish life in France wasn't Paris, it was Provence**... thanks to the Pope!

As in many places, Jews have long been subject to persecution in France. In the Middle Ages, French Jews were the victims of murders, riots, and outright expulsions. There were few places where they were allowed to live, even fewer jobs they were allowed to hold, and many were forced to wear a yellow star.

Life was intolerable... but hope beckoned in the south.

Popes had long owned land in Provence, and the papacy even moved to Avignon* in the 14th century. Next to Avignon was a papal territory called the *Comtat Venaissin* and together they formed the French Papal States. It was here that Jews found refuge†.

Living under the Pope's protection, they became known as *les Juifs du Pape* (the Pope's Jews) and were able to live with far fewer restrictions than in other places. The community thrived, building synagogues and kosher bakeries at a time when they were disappearing elsewhere in France. A new dialect even developed, called *shuadit*, a mixture of Hebrew and Provençal.

Unfortunately, anti-Semitism never dies and over time new restrictions were added in the French Papal States, so that by the late Middle Ages Jews were allowed to live in only four cities. Even there, they were forced into small ghettos, with gates that shut them in at night.

It is in these four cities—Avignon, Carpentras, Cavaillon, and l'Isle-sur-la-Sorgue—that you can find many of the oldest Jewish sites in Provence today. Carpentras, for example, is the home to **France's oldest synagogue**‡ § built in 1343, while Cavaillon's Musée Jouve et Juif Comtadin⸗ ** includes the remnants of a matzo bakery plus Torah scrolls and other historical artifacts.

---

*     tinyurl.com/uxdsevb2
†     tinyurl.com/yclts7v7
‡     tinyurl.com/arrbds77
§     tinyurl.com/3vtwfna6
⸗     tinyurl.com/yhjw2wcm
**   tinyurl.com/n8xzy6hc

Thanks to the French Revolution, Jews were finally granted full citizenship and many restrictions on employment were removed. A process of emigration to other parts of France began and today the majority of French Jews live in and near Paris.

Besides the former French Papal States, Marseille and Nice have large and active Jewish communities and impressive Grand Synagogues. Many towns in Provence also display signs like *Place de la Juiverie* (Jewish Square) or *Rue des Juifs* (Jewish Street) marking their long-ago Jewish neighborhoods. There is a peaceful Jewish cemetery in St-Rémy[*][†] that dates back to the 15th century. It is enclosed by a wall and only open once a year, but you can look through the gate to see inside.

Explore France has put together a helpful guide[‡] to **visiting Jewish sites in Provence**, including directions for a driving tour.

---

[*]   tinyurl.com/cyk7md9n
[†]   tinyurl.com/ne36nwhk
[‡]   tinyurl.com/yx7ar7pu

# Favorite Views

Val and I love beautiful views, and there are a lot of them in Provence. You'll find my descriptions throughout this book, but I thought I would bring them all together in one place in case you as big a fan as I am. Here you go!

## Glanum

From the highest point in the ancient Roman city of Glanum, you have excellent views of St-Rémy and the surrounding area. (page 69)

## La Caume

From one of the highest points in the Alpilles, you can see a very long way. (page 118)

## View *from* Les Baux-de-Provence

The mountaintop fortress of Les Baux sits above the town, with outstanding views over the countryside below. (page 91)

## View *of* Les Baux-de-Provence

From a spot next to a road in the Alpilles, you can look straight across to Les Baux. (page 124)

## View *above* Les Baux-de-Provence

Not far from the viewpoint just mentioned, there is an even higher point with one of the most magnificent views in Provence. You can see for miles in all directions. (page 124)

## Parkplatz Klettern

I have no idea why this place has a German name, but you can often see mountain climbers scaling the steep stone faces of the Alpilles from here. (page 116)

## The Best View of Avignon

In the middle of the Rhône River is an island facing Avignon, with nothing to block your view of this beautiful city. A great place for a picnic or a meal at a riverside restaurant. (page 132)

## Gordes Photo Spot

As you approach this famous hilltop village, there's a specially-designed place for taking photos of it. A selfie hotspot! (page 141)

## Senanque Abbey

Is there anything more beautiful than this serene Cistercian abbey with a lavender field in front of it? (page 142)

## Lunch in Bonnieux

I have a favorite café where I eat lunch in this hilltop village, with views over the Luberon Valley. (page 145)

## Picnic in the Sky

Way above Bonnieux is the Cedar Forest, with incredible views of the Luberon Valley from a secret picnic spot. (page 145)

## Drinks in Lacoste

Facing Bonnieux across the Luberon Valley is the Café de France in Lacoste, a great place for a meal or a drink with a view. (page 147)

## Gigondas Wine Country

Above the wine village of Gigondas is a hiking path and a high viewing platform where you can see vines in all directions. (page 157)

## Mont Sainte-Victoire

Below this beautiful mountain near Aix-en-Provence is a hiking trail with great views of the area. (page 165)

## The Calanques

Take a boat ride and see these rugged "French fjords" towering above the Mediterranean Sea. (page 171)

## Gorge d'Ardeche

The views from the D290 road through this gorge are spectacular, but the drive is death-defying. Not for the faint of heart. (page 167)

# Resources

## Guidebooks and Maps

For a guidebook to Provence that covers all the bases—sights, restaurants, hotels, and the rest—it's hard to beat the one from Rick Steves. Other good guides include Lonely Planet and Fodor's. I also like the Michelin guide, which is especially good on things to see and the history behind them.

If you want a paper map to supplement your GPS, the gold standard is Michelin. They have a wide variety of excellent maps, like the one that covers all of Provence*, or others that cover only a specific region. You can buy them ahead of your trip, or at a bookstore after you arrive in France.

---

\*    tinyurl.com/hwhejw48

# Markets

One of the glories of Provence is its outdoor markets, and the essential guide is Marjorie Williams' *Markets of Provence*[*]. It's a handy little book with everything you need to enjoy the markets to the fullest.

It is also important to have a list of market days in Provence, showing which towns have markets on each day. Below is a list of some of the most important markets, and you can find more information here[†].

**In general, markets take place in the morning from about 8am to noon.**

## Markets Every Day

Aix-en-Provence has a market every morning in Place Richelme (food) and Place de l'Hôtel de Ville (flowers), plus a larger "everything" market throughout town on Tuesday, Thursday, and Saturday mornings.

Avignon has an indoor market at les Halles every morning except Monday.

Velleron has a producer's market every evening except Sunday, starting at 6pm, from April through September. Hours are more limited the rest of the year.

---

[*]    tinyurl.com/2fjfkvre
[†]    tinyurl.com/2ukrzz67

## Monday markets

Cadenet
Forcalquier

## Tuesday markets

Aix-en-Provence
Cucuron
Gordes
Vaison-la-Romaine

## Wednesday markets

Saint-Rémy-de-Provence
Sault

## Thursday markets

Aix-en-Provence
Maussane-les-Alpilles
Orange
Roussillon

## Friday markets

Bonnieux
Carpentras
Eygalières
Lourmarin

## Saturday markets

Aix-en-Provence
Apt
Arles
Uzès

## Sunday markets

L'Isle-sur-la-Sorgue

# Helpful Websites

## Life in Provence*

No surprise, I'm rather fond of my own website.

## Perfectly Provence†

Nothing covers this region like Perfectly Provence. It is the creation of Carolyne Kauser-Abbott, a Canadian who lives part of the year in Provence. I especially like its section on Provençal food‡, which has tons of recipes§.

---

* tinyurl.com/6av84vk9
† tinyurl.com/5sxrt2tf
‡ tinyurl.com/e282bk2n
§ tinyurl.com/8u7rupz4

## The Good Life France[*]

Run by the British transplant Janine Marsh, who lives in "middle-of-nowhere" France, this is one of the most popular French-themed websites out there. It covers everything you want to know about the country, with a strong section on Provence[†].

## France Travel Tips[‡]

The author of this site, Canadian Janice Chung, has been to France dozens of times, and many of her trips have been to Provence. She seeks out unusual experiences, so her site is a great place to learn about "off the beaten track" adventures. Her site has a cool map[§] that allows you to click on a spot to learn more.

## My French Life[¶] and France Today[**]

These are the two of the most popular French-themed websites out there. Both cover France generally, rather than being specific to Provence, but I always love reading their articles. *My French Life* has an especially friendly and active Facebook Group[††].

---

[*] tinyurl.com/4y7845ap
[†] tinyurl.com/5xyx38j2
[‡] tinyurl.com/3bawf7wu
[§] tinyurl.com/cvrvauc2
[¶] tinyurl.com/wnwx4tw7
[**] tinyurl.com/yrnym4kf
[††] tinyurl.com/s9madb7d

## Frenchly[*]

This is a terrific website about all things French, with a particular focus on travel, culture, style, and food and wine.

## Belle Provence Travels[†]

Author Tuula Rampont is an American woman married to a French man, living with their daughter in a village on the Mediterranean coast. She writes about her daily life, and every post is like a sweet little visit to Provence.

# Language

## Dictionary

I love the Larousse French / English dictionary app[‡] and use it all the time.

## Translation

The Google Translate app[§] works remarkably well, and has a great camera feature that lets you read things that are written in another language. You tell the app what language you are trying to read, hit the little camera

---

[*] tinyurl.com/4c5j9y6m
[†] tinyurl.com/3pb8rj59
[‡] tinyurl.com/5a7xp5a9
[§] tinyurl.com/3f95jszn

icon, then point your camera at the text. After a few seconds the original text disappears and is replaced by an English translation. It's like magic!

## Pronunciation

If you want to know how to pronounce a word, Forvo[*] is for you. It has a database of thousands of native speakers pronouncing zillions of words. You enter the word, plus the language it is in, and you are given a choice of speakers who pronounce it for you. Very helpful.

## Art Walks

There are a number of different art walks[†] throughout Provence. Some follow in the footsteps of painters like van Gogh and Cézanne, others allow you to see more contemporary artworks.

## Hiking and Biking

Chemin des Parcs[‡] offers hundreds of hiking and biking routes throughout Provence.

---

[*]   tinyurl.com/cyvkawvj
[†]   tinyurl.com/exhknmky
[‡]   tinyurl.com/4aascnmy

Provence-Cycling* has dozens of bike routes in the Vaucluse region of Provence. A detailed map of each route can be downloaded (go to the bottom of the description.)

* tinyurl.com/fkyy2hzm

# Acknowledgments

My love of travel started early. Every summer my parents would pack up the family and light out for parts unknown. We would roam the American West for weeks, camping in state parks and national forests. My desire to explore the world started there and hasn't stopped yet. Thanks Mom and Dad.

Many people read this book as it was coming together, sharing their advice, and each of them has made it better. My thanks to Leslie Bottorff, Bill Ellig, Scott Gibson, Kristin Harms, Elizabeth Mori, and Steve "Mr. Cartography" Timmerman. Special thanks to Judith Roffman, who test-drove this book on a trip to Provence and provided many invaluable suggestions.

The whimsical illustrations are thanks to the talented Anthony Genilo, and the wonderful cover is by expert designer Greg Abel of gregabeldesign.com. Val took the cover photo at one of our favorite restaurants.

I have the pleasure of writing for some marvelous publications devoted to France, and many of those articles informed this book. I'd like to thank Annette

Charlton of *A French Collection*, Janice Chung of *France Travel Tips*, Carolyne Kauser-Abbott of *Perfectly Provence*, Ariane Laurent-Smith of *France Today*, Judy MacMahon of *MyFrenchLife*, Janine Marsh of *The Good Life France*, Mary Nicklin of *Bonjour Paris*, and Caitlin Shetterly of *Frenchly*.

Having the ability to speak French enriches my life, and for that I'd like to thank my excellent teachers Gisèle Filiol, Marjorie Hamelin and Malika Labidi. I'd also like to thank the members of my French book clubs for expanding my knowledge of French literature, and my language partners for patiently helping me to master this most beautiful of languages.

Many of the things I describe in this book would be unknown to me if not for my wonderful French friends. They have taken Val and me under their wings and helped us discover the real Provence. *Merci beaucoup, chers amis.*

My last and greatest thanks go to my wife Val. It's at her prodding that we moved to Switzerland, at her initiative that we moved to Provence, and she's the one who inspired me to learn French. My life is immeasurably better because of her. *Valou, je t'adore.*

# About the Author

Val and I first visited Provence in 1994 and it was love at first sight. We came back every chance we got, and in 2008 we began a part-time life here. Now we split our time between Provence and California.

It was challenging at first because our French wasn't very good (mine could generously be described as laughable.) But after hard work and plenty of mistakes, we can now speak the language reasonably well and have a wonderful circle of French friends.

Over the years, we've traveled all over Provence, visiting sights both well-known and obscure. So, while we've seen the famous lavender fields and Roman arenas, we've also seen Provence's medieval Plague Wall and learned about its rich Jewish history.

Our French friends have generously introduced us to regional specialties and taught us local expressions (some more polite than others.) They've taken us to their favorite restaurants and shown us hidden picnic spots, and together we've tasted more wine than I care to admit.

My first book, *One Sip at a Time: Learning to Live in Provence*[*], describes the many misadventures of Val and me during our first few years here. It was an Amazon best-seller so I wrote a sequel, *Are We French Yet?*[†] I hope that this latest book will help you make the most of this wonderful corner of France.

I'm a regular contributor to publications like *Perfectly Provence*, *France Today*, *The Good Life France*, *My French Life*, *Frenchly*, and *Bonjour Paris*. You can read my stories on my website, Life in Provence, and follow me on Facebook at @onesip[‡].

---

[*]  tinyurl.com/4ttbhavv
[†]  tinyurl.com/us9n3m5h
[‡]  tinyurl.com/5y9vtw9w